all*you

Delicious
on a *Dime*
Cookbook

Let's cook together!

Have you ever had a meal at someone's house that looked great, tasted amazing and seemed impossibly easy for the cook to make? You can be that cook—all you need is a collection of recipes that take simple, inexpensive ingredients from the supermarket and make them sing.
Welcome to the ALL YOU *Delicious on a Dime Cookbook*. Enjoy!

Beth Lipton
Food Director, ALL YOU

Contents

FOOD STYLING: LYNN MILLER; ANTONIS ACHILLEOS, FOOD STYLING: LYNN MILLER; RYAN BENYI, FOOD STYLING: ANDREA STEINBERG; CHARLES SCHILLER, FOOD STYLING: LYNN MILLER; [...] FOOD STYLING: LYNN MILLER; [...] SAM WILLIAMS, JOHN MONTANA, FOOD STYLING: LYNN MILLER

Multigrain Pancakes

Breakfast

Corn and Cheddar Waffles

cup, whisk together milk, egg and butter. Pour milk mixture into flour mixture and stir until just combined. Fold in corn and cheese.

2 Mist waffle iron with cooking spray. Pour batter onto iron and spread to edges with a spatula. Cook until waffles are golden, 5 to 7 minutes. Transfer to an ovenproof plate, loosely cover with foil and keep warm in oven. Repeat with remaining batter, misting iron with cooking spray before each new batch.

PER SERVING: 521 Cal., 26g Fat (15g Sat.), 127mg Chol., 2g Fiber, 17g Pro., 57g Carb., 664mg Sod.

Kitchen tips

✳ **Serve well.** Enjoy these waffles with maple syrup, or go Southwestern and try them with tomato salsa. Melon or another fresh fruit rounds out the meal.

✳ **Keep extras.** If you have waffles left over, wrap and freeze them. Reheat them in your toaster oven.

Prep: 10 min.

Cook: 7 min. per batch

Serves: 4

Cost per serving:

96¢

- 1 cup all-purpose flour
- ½ cup yellow cornmeal
- 1½ tsp. baking powder
- ½ tsp. salt
- 1 Tbsp. sugar
- 1½ cups milk
- 1 large egg
- 4 Tbsp. unsalted butter, melted and cooled
- 1 cup fresh corn kernels (from 1 large

ear) or 1 cup frozen corn kernels, thawed
- 1 cup grated Cheddar

1 Preheat oven to 200°F and preheat waffle iron. In a large bowl, whisk together flour, cornmeal, baking powder, salt and sugar. In a glass measuring

Migas

Prep: 10 min.

Cook: 10 min.

Serves: 4

Cost per serving:

$1.14

- 6 large eggs
- ¼ cup milk
- Salt
- 2 Tbsp. vegetable oil
- 3 6-inch corn tortillas, cut into ¼-inch strips

- ½ green bell pepper, seeded and diced
- 1 small yellow onion, finely chopped
- 1 clove garlic, finely chopped
- 1 medium tomato, seeded and diced
- 3 oz. grated Cheddar

1 In a medium bowl, whisk together eggs, milk and salt; set aside.

2 Warm oil in a large nonstick skillet over medium-high heat. Add tortilla strips and cook, stirring occasionally, until tortilla strips begin to crisp, about 2 minutes. Add pepper and onion and sauté until softened, about 3 minutes. Add garlic to skillet; sauté 1 minute longer.

3 Add egg mixture, tomato and cheese to skillet. Cook, stirring with a spatula, scraping up cooked eggs and allowing liquid to flow underneath, until eggs are set, 2 to 3 minutes. Serve hot.

PER SERVING: 353 Cal., 24g Fat (8g Sat.), 341mg Chol., 2g Fiber, 18g Pro., 17g Carb., 682mg Sod.

Kitchen tip

❋ **Make it yours.** This is a flexible recipe, so go ahead and experiment with ingredients. Add a seeded, diced jalapeño for a kick, or try a different cheese.

Mini Blueberry Muffins

Prep: 10 min.

Bake: 20 min.

Yield: 48 muffins

Cost per serving:

24¢

- 2¼ cups all-purpose flour
- 1½ tsp. baking powder
- ½ tsp. cinnamon
- ½ tsp. salt
- 2 large eggs
- ¾ cup milk
- ⅔ cup vegetable oil
- 1¼ cups sugar
- 1 tsp. vanilla extract
- 1 cup blueberries (fresh or frozen)

1 Preheat oven to 375°F. Mist 2 24-cup miniature-muffin tins with cooking spray.

2 In a small bowl, mix flour, baking powder, cinnamon and salt. In a separate bowl, whisk eggs, milk, oil, sugar and vanilla. Stir flour mixture into milk mixture. Fold in berries. Spoon batter into muffin cups until ¾ full.

3 Bake until a toothpick inserted into center of a muffin comes out clean, 15 to 20 minutes. Let cool in pans on wire racks for 5 minutes, then turn muffins out onto racks. Serve muffins warm or at room temperature.

PER SERVING (2 MUFFINS): 155 Cal., 7g Fat (1g Sat.), 19mg Chol., 1g Fiber, 2g Pro., 21g Carb., 77mg Sod.

Sausage and Cheddar Grits with Eggs

Prep: 10 min.
Cook: 30 min.
Serves: 4
Cost per serving:

$1.10

- **Salt and pepper**
- **½ cup white or yellow stone-ground grits**
- **7 or 8 links bulk pork breakfast sausage (about 8 oz. total)**
- **¾ cup packed sharp Cheddar, coarsely shredded**
- **4 large eggs**

1 In a medium saucepan, bring 2½ cups water to a boil over high heat. Add ⅛ tsp. salt, reduce heat to medium and slowly whisk in grits. Cook, uncovered, stirring frequently, until grits are tender and thickened, about 20 minutes.

2 Using a sharp paring knife, cut off ends of sausage casings. Squeeze out sausage meat and discard casings. Cook sausage in a medium skillet over medium-high heat, stirring occasionally with a wooden spoon to break up any large pieces, until sausage is fully cooked, about 5 minutes. Remove sausage from skillet with a slotted spoon; set aside. Leave any accumulated fat in skillet.

3 Remove grits from heat and stir in shredded Cheddar and cooked sausage.

4 Return skillet to medium-high heat. Working one at a time, carefully crack eggs into skillet. Cook eggs until whites are set but yolks are still slightly runny, about 3 minutes. (For firmer yolks, flip eggs and cook for 1 minute longer.) Divide grits mixture among 4 plates and top each serving with an egg. Season with salt and pepper and serve.

PER SERVING: 317 Cal., 19g Fat (9g Sat.), 254mg Chol., 1g Fiber, 18g Pro., 17g Carb., 847mg Sod.

Kitchen tip

✳ **Take shortcuts.**
In a hurry? You can use quick-cooking or instant grits. They're less hearty than traditional grits, but they're still tasty. Brown precooked sausage instead of using raw.

Pear-Ginger Muffins

Prep: 25 min.
Bake: 20 min.
Yield: 15 muffins
Cost per serving:

53¢

- 2 cups all-purpose flour
- ¾ cup packed dark brown sugar
- 1 Tbsp. ground ginger
- 2 tsp. baking powder
- 1 tsp. baking soda
- ½ tsp. salt
- ¾ cup buttermilk
- 8 Tbsp. (1 stick) unsalted butter, melted and cooled
- 2 large eggs, lightly beaten
- 1 tsp. vanilla extract
- 2 tsp. grated fresh ginger
- 2 ripe but firm Bosc pears (about 6 oz. each), peeled, cored, diced
- ½ cup chopped pecans

1 Preheat oven to 350°F. Line a 12-cup muffin tin and 3 cups of a 6-cup muffin tin with paper liners.

2 In a large bowl, whisk flour, sugar, ground ginger, baking powder, baking soda and salt. In a medium bowl, whisk buttermilk, melted butter, eggs, vanilla and fresh ginger until blended. Pour into flour mixture and stir until just combined. Do not overmix. Fold in pears and pecans.

3 Divide batter evenly among muffin cups. Bake until tops are golden and a toothpick inserted into center of a muffin comes out clean, about 20 minutes.
PER SERVING (1 MUFFIN): 165 Cal., 10g Fat (4g Sat.), 42mg Chol., 2g Fiber, 4g Pro., 29g Carb., 238mg Sod.

Kitchen tips

Go nuts. Hazelnuts and walnuts work equally well in these muffins.

Swap fruit. Try firm, sweet apples such as Rome instead of pears, if you like.

Banana-Stuffed French Toast

Prep: 20 min.
Cook: 16 min.
Serves: 8
Cost per serving:

$1.32

- 16 slices cinnamon-raisin bread
- ½ cup whipped cream cheese
- 4 large bananas, peeled and thinly sliced
- 6 large eggs
- ¾ cup milk
- 1 tsp. vanilla extract
- Pinch of salt
- 4 Tbsp. (½ stick) unsalted butter
- ½ cup maple syrup, warmed, for serving

1 Preheat oven to 225°F. Lay 8 slices of bread on a work surface and spread one side of each with cream cheese.

Top each with slightly overlapping banana slices. Cover with remaining bread to make sandwiches.

2 In a shallow bowl, beat eggs, milk, vanilla and salt with a fork. Melt 2 Tbsp. butter in a large nonstick skillet over medium heat. Dip 4 sandwiches into egg mixture, turning to soak both sides. Lay sandwiches in skillet and cook for 5 minutes. Flip and cook until browned, about 3 minutes longer. Keep sandwiches warm on an ovenproof plate in oven. Repeat with remaining butter and sandwiches. Serve hot with warm maple syrup.
PER SERVING: 416 Cal., 17g Fat (8g Sat.), 192mg Chol., 4g Fiber, 11g Pro., 59g Carb., 331mg Sod.

Pear-Ginger Muffins

CHARLES SCHILLER. FOOD STYLING: TRACEY SEAMAN. PROP STYLING: GINA PROVENZANO

Kitchen tips

❋ **Swap fruit.**
Currants are sweet and delicate in these scones, but raisins, dried cranberries or chopped dried cherries also work well.

❋ **Make them fresh.**
Scones are best enjoyed the day they're made. Serve them with jam and whipped butter.

Old-Fashioned Cream Scones

Prep: 15 min.
Bake: 20 min.
Yield: 7 scones
Cost per serving:

61¢

- **2 cups cake flour**
- **¼ cup plus 1 Tbsp. sugar**
- **1½ tsp. baking powder**
- **½ tsp. salt**
- **6 Tbsp. cold unsalted butter, cut into small pieces**
- **½ cup dried currants**
- **⅔ cup plus 1 Tbsp. heavy cream**
- **2 large egg yolks**

1 Preheat oven to 400°F. Line a baking sheet with parchment or mist with cooking spray.

2 In a large bowl, whisk flour, ¼ cup sugar, baking powder and salt. Work in butter with fingertips or a pastry cutter until mixture resembles coarse crumbs. Toss in currants.

3 In a small bowl, whisk ⅔ cup cream and yolks; stir into flour mixture with a fork until dough comes together in a ball. Knead dough in bowl three times to blend; do not overwork. On a lightly floured surface, pat dough into a ¾-inch-thick round. Using a 3-inch cutter, cut out scones and transfer to baking sheet. Reshape remaining dough scraps and cut out more scones. Brush scones with remaining 1 Tbsp. cream and sprinkle with remaining 1 Tbsp. sugar.

4 Bake until golden, 15 to 20 minutes. Let cool for 10 minutes before serving.

PER SERVING (1 SCONE):
404 Cal., 21g Fat (12g Sat.), 122mg Chol., 1g Fiber, 5g Pro., 49g Carb., 266mg Sod.

Asparagus Frittata

prepared pan in a circular pattern. Sprinkle cheese on top.

2 Melt butter in skillet over medium heat; add shallot and sauté until softened, about 5 minutes. Transfer shallot to a bowl; add eggs, half-and-half, salt and pepper and whisk to combine. Pour over asparagus and cheese.

3 Bake omelet until puffed and golden, about 40 minutes. Cut into wedges; serve.

PER SERVING: 228 Cal., 18g Fat (6g Sat.), 220mg Chol., 2g Fiber, 11g Pro., 8g Carb., 335mg Sod.

Kitchen tip

✳ **Try another taste.** You can modify this recipe in a few ways to suit your tastes. Instead of Havarti, use Gruyère, Fontina or Parmesan—or even a few dollops of cream cheese. Swap a finely chopped leek or scallions for the shallot. Toss in fresh herbs, like chives or parsley, if you have them.

Prep: 15 min.
Bake: 40 min.
Serves: 6
Cost per serving:
$1.21

- 1 lb. pencil-thin asparagus, ends trimmed
- 3 oz. Havarti, cubed
- 1 Tbsp. unsalted butter
- 1 shallot, chopped
- 5 large eggs
- 1⅓ cups half-and-half
- ¼ tsp. salt
- ¼ tsp. pepper

1 Preheat oven to 350°F. Grease a 9-inch quiche or pie pan. Bring 1 inch water to a boil in a skillet. Add asparagus and cook until crisp-tender, 2 to 3 minutes. Drain, rinse with cold water and pat dry with a clean kitchen towel. Arrange asparagus in

Whole-Wheat Banana Muffins

Prep: 15 min.
Bake: 20 min.
Yield: 12 muffins
Cost per serving:

22¢

- 1½ cups whole-wheat flour
- ½ cup all-purpose flour
- 1½ tsp. baking powder
- ¼ tsp. cinnamon
- ¼ tsp. salt
- 3 large ripe bananas, mashed
- 2 large eggs, lightly beaten
- ¾ cup packed light brown sugar
- ⅓ cup milk
- 3 Tbsp. unsalted butter, melted and cooled
- 1 tsp. vanilla extract
- 12 dried banana chips, optional

1 Preheat oven to 375°F. Mist a standard 12-cup muffin tin with cooking spray or line with paper or foil liners. In a large bowl, whisk both types of flour with baking powder, cinnamon and salt.

2 In a separate bowl, whisk bananas, eggs, sugar, milk, butter and vanilla until smooth. Fold banana mixture into flour mixture until just combined; do not overmix (batter may be lumpy).

3 Spoon batter into prepared muffin cups; top each with a banana chip, if desired. Bake until a toothpick inserted into center of a muffin comes out clean, 18 to 20 minutes. Let cool in tin on a wire rack for 10 minutes, then turn out onto rack to cool completely.

PER SERVING (1 MUFFIN): 189 Cal., 4g Fat (2g Sat.), 44mg Chol., 3g Fiber, 4g Pro., 35g Carb., 102mg Sod.

Kitchen tip

※ **Spot the best bananas.** Be sure to use very ripe bananas, preferably soft ones with brown spots.

Multigrain Pancakes

Prep: 10 min.

Cook: 3 min.
per batch

Yield: about
12 pancakes

Cost per serving:

48¢

- **¾ cup whole-wheat flour**
- **¼ cup all-purpose flour**
- **½ cup quick-cooking oats**
- **2 Tbsp. cornmeal**
- **2 Tbsp. packed dark brown sugar**
- **1 tsp. baking powder**
- **½ tsp. baking soda**
- **¼ tsp. salt**
- **1 cup whole milk**
- **¼ cup plain yogurt**
- **1 Tbsp. unsalted butter, melted and cooled**
- **1 large egg, lightly beaten**
- **1 tsp. vanilla extract**

1 Preheat oven to 200°F. In a large bowl, whisk together whole-wheat and all-purpose flours, oats, cornmeal, brown sugar, baking powder, baking soda and salt. In a small bowl, whisk together milk, yogurt, melted butter, egg and vanilla; stir into flour mixture until just combined (batter should be slightly lumpy).

2 Preheat a large skillet or griddle to medium and mist with cooking spray. Pour batter ¼ cup at a time, spreading gently. Cook until bubbles form on tops of pancakes and bottoms are light golden, about 2 minutes. Flip pancakes; cook until light golden on other side and cooked through, about 1 minute longer. Keep pancakes warm on an ovenproof plate in oven while cooking remaining pancakes.

**PER SERVING
(3 PANCAKES):** 279 Cal.,
8g Fat (4g Sat.), 69mg Chol.,
4g Fiber, 10g Pro., 43g Carb.,
448mg Sod.

Spiced Applesauce

Spiced Applesauce

Prep: 20 min.
Cook: 25 min.
Yield: 4 cups
Cost per serving:

54¢

- 2 lb. firm apples such as Honeycrisp (about 4), peeled, cored, roughly chopped
- ¾ cup orange juice
- ½ tsp. cinnamon
- 1 tsp. ground ginger
- ⅛ tsp. nutmeg
- ⅛ tsp. ground cloves
- Pinch of salt
- 1 tsp. grated fresh ginger
- ¼ cup lightly packed dark brown sugar

1 In a medium saucepan, combine all ingredients; bring to a low boil over medium heat, stirring often.

2 Reduce heat to low, cover saucepan and simmer, stirring occasionally, until apples are tender, about 25 minutes. Let cool for 5 minutes, mash with a potato masher and serve.
PER SERVING (½ CUP): 87 Cal., 0g Fat (0g Sat.), 0mg Chol., 2g Fiber, 1g Pro., 22g Carb., 22mg Sod.

Kitchen tips

✳ **Serve well.** Enjoy this sauce with plain yogurt or on hot oatmeal. Or, spoon it over ice cream as dessert. It also partners beautifully with pork chops for dinner.

✳ **Mix and match.** Try a variety of apples in the sauce for a different taste. Granny Smith, Gala, McIntosh and Golden Delicious are all excellent options.

Cheddar-Spinach Omelet and Toast

Prep: 5 min.
Cook: 10 min.
Serves: 1
Cost per serving:

$1.59

- 2 tsp. olive oil
- ½ cup baby spinach
- 1 large egg plus 2 large egg whites, beaten
- 1 slice 2 percent Cheddar
- Pepper
- 2 slices whole-grain bread, toasted

Warm oil in a skillet over medium heat and sauté spinach until wilted, about 3 minutes.

Pour eggs and egg whites on top of spinach; cook without stirring until eggs are firm, about 4 minutes. Top with cheese, season with pepper and fold. Serve with toast.
PER SERVING: 440 Cal., 20g Fat (4g Sat.), 192mg Chol., 7g Fiber, 29g Pro., 42g Carb., 634mg Sod.

Kitchen tip

✳ **Feed a crowd.** If you're preparing this omelet for more than one person, you can simply multiply the ingredients and scramble them all together.

Overnight Peaches-and-Cream French Toast

and refrigerate for at least 8 hours or overnight.

3 Remove baking dish from refrigerator 30 minutes before baking. Preheat oven to 350°F. Pour cream into a small pan; bring to a boil over high heat. Cook until reduced by half, about 10 minutes. Drizzle over peaches and bake, uncovered, until casserole is lightly browned on top and just cooked through, 45 to 55 minutes. Let stand for 10 minutes before serving.

PER SERVING: 461 Cal., 17g Fat (8g Sat.), 283mg Chol., 2g Fiber, 15g Pro., 63g Carb., 395mg Sod.

Prep: 20 min.

Chill: 8 hr.

Stand: 30 min.

Bake: 55 min.

Serves: 6

Cost per serving:

$1.21

- **1 8-oz. loaf French bread, sliced**
- **8 large eggs**
- **2 cups whole milk**
- **¼ cup sugar**
- **1 tsp. vanilla extract**
- **2 15-oz. cans sliced peaches packed in juice, drained**
- **½ cup packed dark brown sugar**
- **½ tsp. cinnamon**
- **½ cup heavy cream**

1 Butter a 9-by-13-inch baking dish. Arrange bread in a tight, flat layer in dish.

2 In a large bowl, whisk together eggs with milk, sugar and vanilla until blended; pour over bread. Arrange peaches on top and sprinkle with brown sugar and cinnamon. Cover baking dish tightly

---

Kitchen tip

❋ **Get a head start.** This is a great dish to make if you're having guests for breakfast. Prepare it the night before, cover and refrigerate. Bring to room temperature in the morning before baking. Serve warm with bacon or sausage on the side.

Kitchen tips

✳ **Add another layer.** Shred a bit of sharp Cheddar into the batter for an even heartier and more decadent treat. Swap brown sugar or honey for the maple syrup, if you like.

✳ **Top it off.** Sauté sliced tart green apples, pears or bananas in a bit of butter and brown sugar to serve with the waffles.

Maple-Bacon Waffles

Prep: 10 min.
Cook: 1 hr.
Yield: 6 waffles
Cost per serving:

$1.03

- **6 slices bacon (about 6 oz.)**
- **6 Tbsp. maple syrup**
- **2 cups all-purpose flour**
- **1 tsp. baking powder**
- **¾ tsp. baking soda**
- **¼ tsp. salt**
- **1⅓ cups buttermilk**
- **4 Tbsp. canola oil**
- **2 large eggs**

1 Preheat oven to 375°F; line a large, rimmed baking sheet with parchment. Lay bacon on sheet and brush both sides with 2 Tbsp. maple syrup. Bake, turning once, until crisp and browned, 20 to 25 minutes. Discard fat and lower oven temperature to 200°F. Coarsely chop bacon.

2 In a large bowl, mix flour, baking powder, baking soda and salt. In a small bowl, whisk together buttermilk, 2 Tbsp. canola oil, eggs and remaining maple syrup. Stir buttermilk mixture into flour mixture and fold in bacon.

3 Preheat a 7-inch waffle iron. Brush with a bit of oil; add about ½ cup batter. Cook until lightly browned and crisp, about 6 minutes. Transfer to an ovenproof plate and keep warm in oven. Repeat with remaining oil and batter.
PER SERVING (1 WAFFLE):
408 Cal., 18g Fat (4g Sat.), 89mg Chol., 1g Fiber, 13g Pro., 49g Carb., 650mg Sod.

Mini Spicy Cheese Muffins

Prep: 20 min.

Bake: 15 min.

Yield: about 24 muffins

Cost per serving:

34¢

- 1 cup all-purpose flour
- 1 cup yellow cornmeal
- 1 Tbsp. baking powder
- 1 tsp. baking soda
- 1 Tbsp. sugar
- ½ tsp. salt
- 2 large eggs, at room temperature
- 1 cup buttermilk, at room temperature
- ¼ cup vegetable oil
- 1 cup grated Monterey Jack
- 2 jalapeños, seeded and chopped (about ¼ cup)

1 Preheat oven to 375°F. Lightly mist 2 12-cup mini-muffin tins with cooking spray.

2 In a bowl, combine flour, cornmeal, baking powder, baking soda, sugar and salt. In a separate bowl, beat eggs with buttermilk and oil. Pour egg mixture into flour mixture and stir to form a thick batter. Fold in cheese and jalapeños.

3 Spoon enough batter to half-fill 24 mini-muffin cups. Bake until a toothpick inserted into center of a muffin comes out clean, about 15 minutes. Cool in pans on wire racks for 5 minutes, then turn muffins out onto racks to cool further. Serve warm or at room temperature.

PER SERVING (2 MUFFINS): 192 Cal., 9g Fat (2g Sat.), 46mg Chol., 1g Fiber, 6g Pro., 22g Carb., 362mg Sod.

Cranberry-Orange Coffee Cake

Prep: 30 min.
Bake: 1 hr. 5 min.
Serves: 12
Cost per serving:

98¢

CAKE:

- 3 cups all-purpose flour
- 1½ tsp. baking powder
- 1 tsp. baking soda
- ½ tsp. salt
- 1½ cups sour cream, at room temperature
- 2 tsp. vanilla extract
- 12 Tbsp. (1½ sticks) unsalted butter, at room temperature
- 1 cup sugar
- ½ cup packed dark brown sugar
- Zest of 1 orange
- 3 large eggs, at room temperature
- ¾ cup chopped toasted pecans
- 1 14-oz. can whole-berry cranberry sauce

GLAZE:

- 1 cup confectioners' sugar
- 1½ Tbsp. orange juice

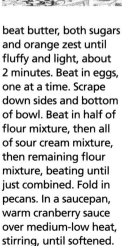

1 Make cake: Preheat oven to 350°F. Grease and flour a 12-cup tube or Bundt pan. In a bowl, whisk flour, baking powder, baking soda and salt. In a separate bowl, mix sour cream and vanilla.

2 In a large bowl, using an electric mixer on medium speed, beat butter, both sugars and orange zest until fluffy and light, about 2 minutes. Beat in eggs, one at a time. Scrape down sides and bottom of bowl. Beat in half of flour mixture, then all of sour cream mixture, then remaining flour mixture, beating until just combined. Fold in pecans. In a saucepan, warm cranberry sauce over medium-low heat, stirring, until softened.

3 Spread ⅓ of batter in pan. Spread ½ of cranberry sauce over. Repeat layers, ending with last ⅓ of batter. Gently run a skewer or thin knife through batter to swirl cranberry sauce in a marble pattern. Bake cake until a skewer inserted in center comes out clean, 55 to 65 minutes. Let cake cool in pan on a wire rack for 10 minutes; unmold onto rack to cool completely.

4 Make glaze: When cake is cool, whisk together confectioners' sugar and juice until glaze is smooth and has desired consistency (add more juice or sugar if glaze is too thick or thin). Drizzle glaze over cake. Let stand until glaze sets, about 10 minutes.

PER SERVING: 519 Cal., 23g Fat (12g Sat.), 103mg Chol., 2g Fiber, 7g Pro., 73g Carb., 319mg Sod.

Dutch Baby Apple Pancake

Prep: 20 min.
Bake: 30 min.
Serves: 4
Cost per serving:

$1.11

- ½ cup half-and-half
- 3 large eggs
- ½ tsp. vanilla extract
- 6 Tbsp. unsalted butter, melted
- ¼ tsp. salt

- ½ cup all-purpose flour
- ½ tsp. cinnamon
- 3 Tbsp. packed light brown sugar
- 2 Tbsp. lemon juice
- 2 Granny Smith apples, peeled, cored and sliced
- ¼ cup chopped walnuts, optional
- Confectioners' sugar, optional

1 Preheat oven to 375°F. In a blender, process half-and-half, eggs, vanilla and 2 Tbsp. butter until smooth. Blend in salt, flour and ¼ tsp. cinnamon.

2 In a 10-inch nonstick skillet with an ovenproof handle, mix remaining butter and cinnamon with brown sugar and lemon juice. Bring to a boil over medium-high heat, stirring. Stir in apples, reduce heat to low and simmer, stirring often, until apples are tender and liquid has thickened, about 7 minutes.

3 Pour batter over apple mixture; sprinkle with nuts, if desired. Bake until set and top is golden, 25 to 30 minutes. Sprinkle with confectioners' sugar, if desired.

PER SERVING: 373 Cal., 25g Fat (14g Sat.), 216mg Chol., 1g Fiber, 8g Pro., 32g Carb., 213mg Sod.

Coconut-Cranberry Granola

Prep: 10 min.
Bake: 25 min.
Yield: 6 cups
Cost per serving:

56¢

- 3 cups rolled oats
- 1 cup sweetened flaked coconut
- 1 cup raw almonds, roughly chopped
- 2 Tbsp. honey
- ¼ cup packed light brown sugar
- ¼ cup vegetable oil
- 1 tsp. cinnamon
- 1 tsp. salt
- 1 cup dried cranberries

1 Preheat oven to 350°F. In a bowl, mix oats, coconut and almonds. In a microwave-safe bowl, mix honey, brown sugar, oil, cinnamon and salt; microwave on high until sugar begins to dissolve, about 30 seconds. Stir into oat mixture.

2 Spread mixture on a rimmed baking sheet. Bake, stirring twice, until granola is golden brown and toasted, 20 to 25 minutes. Transfer to a bowl. Let cool, stirring occasionally. Toss in cranberries.

PER SERVING (½ CUP): 289 Cal., 15g Fat (4g Sat.), 0mg Chol., 4g Fiber, 6g Pro., 36g Carb., 217mg Sod.

Kitchen tip

✳ **Add dairy.** Try this flavorful granola with plain or vanilla yogurt.

Dutch Baby Apple Pancake

Shrimp Bruschetta

Appetizers

Curried Chicken Salad in Lettuce Cups

Kitchen tips

✳ **Plump the fruit.** If your raisins are dry, place them in a bowl, cover them with boiling water and let stand for 10 minutes. Drain and pat dry before adding to the salad. Swap dried cranberries for the raisins if you prefer.

✳ **Turn over a new leaf.** For a touch of bitter flavor and a pretty splash of purple, swap radicchio for the Boston lettuce. With either type of lettuce, trim larger leaves with kitchen shears to make compact "cups."

Prep: 15 min.
Yield: 16 pieces
Cost per serving:

66¢

- ¼ cup slivered almonds
- 1 cup mayonnaise
- 2 tsp. curry powder
- ½ tsp. paprika
- 3 scallions, white and light green parts only, thinly sliced
- ½ cup golden raisins
- 4 cups shredded roasted chicken, skin and bones removed (from a 3-lb. rotisserie chicken)
- Salt and pepper
- 16 small Boston lettuce leaves

1 Place almonds in a dry skillet over medium heat. Cook, stirring frequently, until just golden brown and fragrant. Remove to a bowl and allow to cool for 5 minutes.

2 Combine mayonnaise, curry powder, paprika, scallions, raisins and almonds in a large bowl. Mix well. Add chicken to bowl with dressing and stir until well coated. Season with salt and pepper.

3 Arrange lettuce leaves on a serving platter. Fill each leaf with 2 Tbsp. chicken salad and serve immediately.

PER SERVING (1 PIECE): 124 Cal., 13g Fat (2g Sat.), 40mg Chol., 1g Fiber, 8g Pro., 5g Carb., 180mg Sod.

Spinach Dip with Crudités

Prep: 5 min.
Serves: 8
Cost per serving:
38¢

- 1 10-oz. package frozen spinach, thawed and squeezed dry
- 2 scallions, white part only, thinly sliced
- ¾ cup reduced-fat mayonnaise
- ¾ cup plain yogurt
- Salt and pepper
- Assorted crudités

Blend spinach, scallions, mayonnaise and yogurt in a food processor until smooth. Season with salt and pepper. Keep covered and chilled until ready to serve. Arrange crudités around dip; serve cold.
PER SERVING: 76 Cal., 4g Fat (1g Sat.), 3mg Chol., 1g Fiber, 3g Pro., 8g Carb., 389mg Sod.

Cheese and Tomato Toasts

Prep: 15 min.
Cook: 5 min.
Serves: 8
Cost per serving:
$1.13

- 5 to 6 oz. mild, creamy goat cheese or cream cheese, at room temperature
- 2 Tbsp. chopped fresh parsley
- ¼ tsp. pepper
- 2 plum tomatoes, seeded and diced
- 3 Tbsp. olive oil
- ⅛ tsp. salt
- 1 loaf (about 8 oz.) Italian bread
- 2 cloves garlic, halved

1 Preheat oven to 400°F. In a small bowl, stir together goat cheese, 1 Tbsp. parsley and pepper until thoroughly combined. In a medium bowl, gently toss tomatoes with 2 tsp. olive oil, salt and 1½ tsp. parsley.

2 Slice off and discard ends of bread. Slice loaf diagonally into ½-inch-thick slices and place on an ungreased baking sheet. Toast in oven until golden brown, about 5 minutes. Rub one side of each toast slice with cut side of garlic. Brush with remaining olive oil.

3 Just before serving, spread toast slices with cheese mixture and top with tomato mixture. Top with remaining 1½ tsp. parsley.
PER SERVING: 173 Cal., 10g Fat (4g Sat.), 8mg Chol., 1g Fiber, 6g Pro., 15g Carb., 262mg Sod.

Kitchen tips

✳ **Get a head start.** You can make the cheese mixture up to a day ahead. Keep it covered and refrigerated. Let it soften at room temperature before spreading.

✳ **Punch it up.** Use an herbed goat cheese for even more flavor.

Mini Ham-Salad Sandwiches

Prep: 15 min.
Yield: 24 pieces
Cost per serving:

32¢

- **2 large eggs**
- **12 oz. lean ham, chopped**
- **¼ cup sweet pickle relish**
- **2 ribs celery, thinly sliced**
- **2 Tbsp. chopped fresh parsley**
- **1 Tbsp. lemon juice**
- **¼ cup mayonnaise**
- **12 thin slices white or whole-wheat sandwich bread, crusts removed**

1 Place eggs in a pot; cover with cold water. Bring to a boil. Remove from heat, cover and let stand for 12 minutes. Rinse with cold water until eggs are cool; peel eggs and chop. Place in a large bowl.

2 Add ham, relish, celery and parsley to bowl. Gently stir in lemon juice and mayonnaise. Spread ⅓ cup ham mixture on 6 slices of bread. Top with remaining bread slices.

3 Cut sandwiches diagonally, then cut each triangle in half.

PER SERVING (1 PIECE): 78 Cal., 3g Fat (1g Sat.), 29mg Chol., 1g Fiber, 5g Pro., 8g Carb., 263mg Sod.

Kitchen tip

✳ **Cut it up.** Chop the ham in a food processor by pulsing several times.

Green-Tomato Salsa

Prep: 15 min.
Chill: 30 min.
Serves: 8
Cost per serving:

$1.06

- **1 lb. green tomatoes or tomatillos, chopped**
- **2 Tbsp. grated onion**
- **1 jalapeño, seeded and minced**
- **½ cup chopped fresh cilantro**
- **2 Tbsp. lime juice**
- **½ tsp. salt**
- **¼ tsp. pepper**
- **2 large avocados, pitted, peeled and cut into chunks**

1 Combine tomatoes, onion, jalapeño, cilantro, lime juice, salt and pepper in a large bowl.

2 Add avocado to bowl and toss ingredients together. Season with additional salt and pepper. Cover and refrigerate for at least 30 minutes before serving. Serve with tortilla chips, if desired.

PER SERVING: 88 Cal., 7g Fat (1g Sat.), 0mg Chol., 4g Fiber, 2g Pro., 7g Carb., 157mg Sod.

Roasted Eggplant Dip

Prep: 30 min.
Cook: 17 min.
Serves: 8
Cost per serving:

99¢

- 1 large eggplant
- 1 Tbsp. lemon juice
- 2 Tbsp. extra-virgin olive oil
- 1 onion, finely chopped
- 1 medium red bell pepper, seeded, finely chopped
- 1 medium green bell pepper, seeded, finely chopped
- 1 jalapeño, seeded, minced
- ¼ tsp. crushed red pepper
- Salt and pepper
- 4 cloves garlic, minced
- 1 cup drained canned petite diced tomatoes
- 1 tsp. red wine vinegar
- 2 Tbsp. chopped fresh parsley
- 2 Tbsp. chopped fresh basil
- 2 Tbsp. grated Parmesan
- Crudités or pita chips, optional

1 Slice eggplant in half lengthwise, cutting through stem. Scoop out pulp, leaving a ¼-inch border. Brush the insides with lemon juice, wrap tightly in plastic wrap and refrigerate.

2 Finely chop eggplant pulp. Warm oil in a large skillet over medium heat. Add eggplant pulp, onion, bell peppers and jalapeño. Sprinkle with crushed red pepper, 1 tsp. salt and ½ tsp. pepper. Sauté until vegetables are tender, about 12 minutes. Add garlic and tomatoes; sauté 5 minutes longer. Let cool 10 minutes, then stir in vinegar, parsley, basil and Parmesan. Transfer to a bowl and let cool completely. (Dip can be made up to 8 hours ahead. Cover and refrigerate.)

3 When cool, taste and season dip with additional salt and pepper. Pat eggplant shells dry and fill with dip. Serve with crudités and pita chips, if desired.
PER SERVING: 72 Cal., 4g Fat (1g Sat.), 1mg Chol., 3g Fiber, 2g Pro., 9g Carb., 255mg Sod.

Chicken Wings with Blue Cheese Dip

Prep: 15 min.
Cook: 40 min.
Chill: 2 hr.
Serves: 10
Cost per serving:

$1.61

DIP:
- 4 oz. crumbled blue cheese
- ¾ cup mayonnaise
- ¼ cup sour cream
- 1 Tbsp. red wine vinegar
- 1 Tbsp. lemon juice
- ¼ tsp. garlic powder
- Salt and pepper

WINGS:
- ¼ cup ketchup
- ¼ cup hot sauce (such as Frank's RedHot)
- ⅓ cup red wine vinegar
- 1 Tbsp. spicy brown mustard
- 1 Tbsp. Worcestershire sauce
- 1 tsp. onion powder
- 1 tsp. garlic powder
- 1 Tbsp. sugar
- 4 Tbsp. unsalted butter
- 3 lb. chicken wings, tips removed, wings separated at joints

1 Make dip: In a bowl, mix blue cheese, mayonnaise, sour cream, vinegar, juice and garlic powder. Season with salt and pepper. Cover and chill for 2 hours.

2 Make wings: Preheat oven to 450°F. Line a large, rimmed baking sheet with foil. Place a cooling rack on top; mist with cooking spray.

3 In a small pan, combine ketchup, hot sauce, vinegar, mustard, Worcestershire sauce, onion powder, garlic powder, sugar and butter. Cook over low heat, stirring, until well combined and smooth. Pour into a bowl and let cool.

4 Pour ¼ cup sauce into a small bowl; cover. In a large bowl, toss wings with ½ cup sauce until coated. Place wings on rack. Roast for 10 minutes; brush with more sauce. Roast 10 minutes longer; brush with sauce. Turn wings over, brush with sauce and roast 10 minutes longer. Brush and roast for a final 10 minutes.

5 Remove wings to a large bowl; toss with reserved sauce. Serve with blue cheese dip.
PER SERVING: 531 Cal., 44g Fat (14g Sat.), 141mg Chol., 0g Fiber, 28g Pro., 5g Carb., 616mg Sod.

Beef Teriyaki Skewers

Soak: 30 min.
Prep: 15 min.
Cook: 8 min.
Yield: 24 skewers
Cost per serving:

84¢

- 1½ lb. beef sirloin, cut into 24 1-inch pieces
- 6 mushrooms, quartered
- 24 cherry tomatoes
- ½ cup canola oil
- ½ tsp. salt
- ¼ tsp. pepper
- ¼ cup packed dark brown sugar
- 3 Tbsp. soy sauce
- 2 tsp. sesame oil
- ¼ cup sesame seeds

1 Soak 24 small bamboo skewers in water for 30 minutes. Preheat broiler to high; line a broiling pan with foil. Place beef, mushrooms and tomatoes in a bowl. Add canola oil, salt and pepper; toss to coat.

2 Thread meat and vegetables onto skewers, alternating.

Lay skewers on pan. Cover handle end with foil to prevent burning.

3 In a small bowl, mix sugar, soy sauce and sesame oil, stirring until sugar has dissolved. Broil skewers, turning, until meat begins to brown, about 3 minutes. Brush liberally with glaze and continue broiling until beef is lightly charred, 2 to 3 minutes longer. Transfer to a platter and sprinkle with sesame seeds. Serve warm.
PER SERVING (1 SKEWER): 111 Cal., 8g Fat (2g Sat.), 20mg Chol., 0g Fiber, 7g Pro., 4g Carb., 186mg Sod.

*Chicken Wings
with Blue Cheese Dip*

Salmon and Dill Spread

spoon or pipe 1 heaping Tbsp. spread onto wide end of each leaf. Serve right away, or cover and chill for up to 6 hours. Garnish with dill sprigs, if desired.

PER SERVING: 159 Cal., 9g Fat (4g Sat.), 37mg Chol., 6g Fiber, 13g Pro., 9g Carb., 472mg Sod.

Kitchen tips

✳ **Get cracking.** Instead of spooning or piping the spread onto the endive, serve it in a bowl with assorted crudités and crackers. Or, try it on radicchio leaves instead of the endive for a burst of color.

✳ **Boost the flavor.** Toss a tablespoon or two of beet horseradish into the food processor when you add the canned salmon. It lends a brighter pink hue and gives the flavor extra depth.

✳ **Try it in the morning.** This spread is also delicious when slathered on bagels. If you're having guests for brunch, make the spread the night before, transfer to a bowl, cover and chill. Serve it in the morning with toasted bagels, sliced red onion, sliced tomatoes and capers.

Prep: 10 min.
Chill: 2 hr.
Serves: 8
Cost per serving:

$2.07

- 1 14.75-oz. can red salmon, drained, skin and bones removed
- 1 tsp. finely grated lemon zest
- 1½ Tbsp. lemon juice
- 8 oz. reduced-fat cream cheese, at room temperature
- 2 oz. smoked salmon, chopped (about ½ cup)
- 2 Tbsp. chopped fresh dill
- Salt and pepper
- 3 heads endive

1 In a food processor, puree canned salmon, lemon juice, lemon zest and cream cheese until smooth, stopping and scraping down sides of work bowl a few times. Add smoked salmon and dill; pulse just to combine, taking care not to puree completely. Taste and season with salt and pepper.

2 Transfer mixture to a bowl, cover and chill for at least 2 hours, or up to 2 days. When ready to serve, separate leaves of endive and

Kitchen tips

✳ **Let everyone build their own.** Instead of making the bruschetta yourself, you can serve the shrimp mixture in a bowl with the bread slices (or crackers) on the side.

✳ **Take it indoors.** You can make this delicious dish any time of year. If it's too cold outside to grill, toast the bread in the toaster oven.

Shrimp Bruschetta

Prep: 10 min.
Cook: 3 min.
Yield: 16 pieces
Cost per serving:

$1.95

- **1 lb. cooked small shrimp, peeled, deveined and chopped (reserve 16 whole for garnish, optional)**
- **2 small tomatoes, cored and chopped (about 1 cup)**
- **2 Tbsp. ketchup**
- **1 Tbsp. packed dark brown sugar**
- **1 clove garlic, chopped**
- **1 Tbsp. chopped fresh parsley**
- **2 Tbsp. olive oil, plus more for brushing**
- **1½ Tbsp. rice vinegar**
- **Salt and pepper**
- **16 slices of French bread**

1 Mix shrimp, tomatoes, ketchup, sugar, garlic and parsley. Add 2 Tbsp. oil and vinegar. Season with salt and pepper. Cover and chill.

2 Preheat grill and set rack 6 inches from heat. Lightly brush one side of each piece of bread with oil. Grill bread, oiled side up, for 1 minute. Turn and grill other side until lightly browned, 1 to 2 minutes.

3 Spoon about a tablespoon of shrimp mixture on oiled side of each bread slice. Garnish with whole shrimp, if desired.

PER SERVING (2 PIECES):
201 Cal., 7g Fat (1g Sat.), 63mg Chol., 2g Fiber, 11g Pro., 24g Carb., 852mg Sod.

Roast Chicken with Potatoes and Shallots

Chicken & Turkey

Orange and Balsamic Chicken Breasts

softened, about 1 minute. Add broth, orange juice, vinegar and sugar; cook, stirring, until slightly reduced, 1 to 2 minutes. Remove skillet from heat, add remaining butter, and stir until thickened. Season with salt. Slice chicken, pour sauce on top and serve.

PER SERVING: 320 Cal., 12g Fat (4g Sat.), 114mg Chol., 0g Fiber, 41g Pro., 11g Carb., 409mg Sod.

Kitchen tips

✳ **Trade onions.** If you don't have a shallot on hand, you can substitute scallions. Use only the white parts, and chop finely.

✳ **Swap meats.** Try this tasty recipe with medallions made from sliced pork tenderloin, pounded to ½-inch thickness.

✳ **Choose sides.** A green vegetable or tossed salad pairs well with this dish. Make it a complete meal with roasted red potatoes or brown rice.

Prep: 5 min.
Cook: 12 min.
Serves: 4
Cost per serving:

$1.81

- 24 oz. boneless, skinless chicken breasts, pounded to ½-inch thickness

- Salt
- ¼ cup all-purpose flour
- 1 Tbsp. vegetable oil
- 2 Tbsp. unsalted butter
- 1 shallot, finely chopped
- ⅓ cup low-sodium chicken broth
- ⅓ cup orange juice
- 1 Tbsp. balsamic vinegar
- 1 tsp. sugar

1 Sprinkle chicken with salt and dredge in flour, shaking off excess.

2 Warm oil and 1 Tbsp. butter in a large skillet over medium-high heat until butter foams. Add chicken; cook until cooked through and golden, turning once, about 8 minutes total. Transfer to a plate and cover with foil.

3 Add shallot to skillet and sauté until

Kitchen tips

✳ **Make it meatless.** To transform this dish into a vegetarian supper, use vegetable broth and toss in cubes of tofu rather than chicken.

✳ **Give it a boost.** Crowd-pleasing fried rice is a great way to introduce brown rice to skeptics. You can start with half brown rice and half white rice and gradually work in more brown over time.

Chicken, Snow Pea and Cashew Fried Rice

Prep: 15 min.
Cook: 11 min.
Serves: 4
Cost per serving:

$2.39

- 1 lb. boneless, skinless chicken breasts, thinly sliced
- ¼ cup teriyaki sauce
- 3 Tbsp. vegetable oil
- 3 scallions, finely chopped
- 2 cloves garlic, finely chopped
- 1 Tbsp. finely chopped fresh ginger
- 8 oz. snow peas, trimmed
- ¼ cup low-sodium chicken broth
- 4 cups cooked white rice
- 3 Tbsp. chopped roasted cashews

1 Combine chicken and 2 Tbsp. teriyaki sauce in a bowl and set aside. Warm 1½ Tbsp. vegetable oil in a wok or large nonstick skillet over high heat. Add chicken and cook, stirring, until no longer pink, 3 to 5 minutes. Transfer to a clean bowl.

2 Add scallions, garlic, ginger and remaining vegetable oil to wok and cook, stirring, for 1 minute. Add snow peas and chicken broth, cover and cook until tender, 2 to 3 minutes. Stir in rice, chicken and remaining 2 Tbsp. teriyaki sauce and cook, stirring, until rice is heated through, 1 to 2 minutes. Top with cashews and serve.

PER SERVING: 508 Cal., 15g Fat (2g Sat.), 66mg Chol., 3g Fiber, 35g Pro., 56g Carb., 470mg Sod.

Pulled-Chicken Sandwiches

Prep: 10 min.
Cook: 5 hr.
Serves: 6
Cost per serving:

$1.89

- **2 onions, thinly sliced**
- **1 lb. boneless, skinless chicken breasts**
- **¾ lb. boneless, skinless chicken thighs**
- **1 cup ketchup**
- **2 Tbsp. cider vinegar**
- **1 Tbsp. Dijon mustard**
- **2 Tbsp. molasses**
- **1 tsp. onion powder**
- **1 tsp. cumin**
- **½ tsp. garlic powder**
- **½ tsp. Tabasco**
- **½ tsp. salt**
- **Whole-wheat hamburger buns, optional**

1 Scatter onions on bottom of slow cooker. Arrange chicken breasts and thighs on top of onions.

2 In a medium bowl, combine ketchup, vinegar, mustard, molasses, onion powder, cumin, garlic powder, Tabasco and salt. Pour mixture over chicken. Cover, set to low and cook until chicken is fork-tender and sauce has thickened, about 5 hours.

3 Remove chicken from slow cooker and shred meat with your fingers. Stir chicken back into sauce. Serve hot, on whole-wheat buns, if desired.

PER SERVING: 232 Cal., 3g Fat (1g Sat.), 91mg Chol., 1g Fiber, 30g Pro., 20g Carb., 805mg Sod.

KATE SEARS; FOOD STYLING: LYNN MILLER

Chicken and Rice Soup

Prep: 15 min.
Cook: 45 min.
Serves: 6
Cost per serving:

$1.70

- **Salt and pepper**
- **½ cup long-grain brown rice, rinsed**
- **2 Tbsp. canola oil**
- **2 carrots, cut into ½-inch dice**
- **1 large onion, chopped**
- **1 rib celery, thinly sliced**
- **1 clove garlic, minced**
- **2 large boneless, skinless chicken breast halves (6 to 8 oz. each), cut into ½-inch dice**
- **6 cups low-sodium chicken broth**
- **1 cup cauliflower florets, cut into small pieces**
- **1 cup broccoli florets, cut into small pieces**
- **½ cup frozen peas, thawed**
- **2 Tbsp. chopped fresh parsley**

1 Bring a large pot of salted water to a boil. Add rice, cover, reduce heat and cook until tender, about 30 minutes. Drain and rinse under cold running water. Set aside.

2 Warm oil in a large pot over medium-high heat. Add carrots, onion and celery; cook, stirring often, until slightly softened, about 3 minutes. Add garlic and cook, stirring, for 1 minute. Add chicken, then broth. Bring to a boil over high heat, then reduce to low. Simmer for about 10 minutes.

3 Add cauliflower, broccoli and peas to soup. Stir in reserved rice. Cook until vegetables are soft, about 10 minutes. Sprinkle with parsley; season with salt and pepper. Serve hot.

PER SERVING: 207 Cal., 6g Fat (0g Sat.), 30mg Chol., 3g Fiber, 18g Pro., 22g Carb., 907mg Sod.

Kitchen tip

✳ **Give it some color.** Swap a 14.5-ounce can of diced tomatoes with their liquid for 1½ cups of broth. Stir in the tomatoes as you're adding the broth.

Curried Chicken Breasts

Prep: 5 min.
Bake: 30 min.
Serves: 4
Cost per serving:

$1.97

- **⅓ cup plain yogurt (not nonfat)**
- **1 Tbsp. olive oil**
- **2 tsp. curry powder**
- **1 tsp. chili powder**
- **1 tsp. lime juice**
- **1 clove garlic, finely chopped**
- **Salt**
- **4 boneless, skinless chicken breast halves**

1 Preheat oven to 375°F. In a small bowl, whisk together yogurt, olive oil, curry powder, chili powder, lime juice and garlic until well combined. Season with salt. Arrange chicken in an 8-inch glass baking dish, pour yogurt mixture evenly on top and turn chicken to coat.

2 Bake until an instant-read thermometer inserted into thickest part of chicken reads 165°F, 25 to 30 minutes. Let stand 5 minutes before serving.

PER SERVING: 207 Cal., 6g Fat (1g Sat.), 85mg Chol., 1g Fiber, 34g Pro., 2g Carb., 544mg Sod.

Kitchen tip

✳ **Fill your plate.** Roasted or mashed sweet potatoes make a great foil for the spice of the curry mixture on the chicken breasts. Don't forget to offer jarred mango chutney on the side. A green veggie such as string beans rounds out the meal.

Chicken and Apple Salad

Prep: 25 min.
Serves: 4
Cost per serving:

$2.80

- **1 3½-lb. rotisserie chicken**
- **2 medium Granny Smith apples, cored, cut into ¼-inch dice**
- **2 Tbsp. fresh lime juice**
- **2 Tbsp. finely chopped red onion**
- **½ cup reduced-fat mayonnaise**
- **2 Tbsp. chopped fresh cilantro**
- **¼ tsp. crushed red pepper**
- **Salt**
- **8 cups mixed salad greens**

1 Remove meat from chicken and dice, discarding skin and bones (you should have about 4 cups of meat).

2 Toss apples with 1 Tbsp. lime juice in a large bowl. Add chicken and red onion. In a separate small bowl, whisk together mayonnaise, cilantro, red pepper, ½ tsp. salt and remaining 1 Tbsp. lime juice. Stir dressing into chicken mixture to coat. Season with salt.

3 Arrange greens on four plates. Top with chicken salad and serve.

PER SERVING: 286 Cal., 10g Fat (2g Sat.), 93mg Chol., 3g Fiber, 32g Pro., 20g Carb., 1,029mg Sod.

Kitchen tips

✳ **Try another apple.** The tang of tart Granny Smith apples is great in this salad, but you can substitute a sweeter variety, if you prefer. Golden Delicious, Gala and Fuji are all good choices.

✳ **Wrap it up.** Roll the salad and greens into whole-wheat tortillas for family-pleasing wraps.

Curried Chicken Breasts

Roast Chicken with Potatoes and Shallots

Prep: 15 min.
Cook: 55 min.
Serves: 4
Cost per serving:

$2.63

- ½ lb. small red potatoes (larger ones cut in half or quarters)
- 6 shallots, halved
- 1 Tbsp. olive oil
- ½ tsp. dried rosemary
- Salt
- 1 Tbsp. soy sauce
- 1 Tbsp. honey
- 1 Tbsp. Dijon mustard
- 4 bone-in, skin-on chicken thigh and leg pieces

1 Preheat oven to 450°F. Line bottom and sides of a 9-by-13-inch baking pan with heavy-duty aluminum foil. In baking pan, toss potatoes and shallots with oil, rosemary and ½ tsp. salt. Roast for 15 to 20 minutes.

2 In a small bowl, combine soy sauce, honey and mustard. Remove baking dish from oven; stir potato mixture. Mist a wire rack with cooking spray; set it on top of baking dish.

3 Place chicken on rack. Brush with soy sauce mixture and roast until an instant-read thermometer registers 165°F when stuck into thickest part of thigh, about 35 minutes (check chicken after 20 minutes; if skin is browning too quickly, tent chicken with foil). Let rest 5 minutes. Serve chicken with potato mixture.
PER SERVING: 394 Cal., 18g Fat (5g Sat.), 79mg Chol., 3g Fiber, 21g Pro., 38g Carb., 692mg Sod.

Turkey Chili Cheese Pie with Cornmeal Crust

sauté until fragrant, about 1 minute. Stir in turkey, mixing well and breaking up large clumps of meat. Stir in tomatoes and broth. Add beans, bring to a boil and pour into slow cooker.

2 In a large bowl, combine flour, cornmeal, baking powder and salt. Mix well, then stir in egg, milk, cheese and ¼ cup vegetable oil. Pour batter over chili in slow cooker and gently spread to cover. Cover slow cooker and cook on low until chili is hot and crust is lightly browned and cooked through, about 5 hours.

PER SERVING: 482 Cal., 24g Fat (6g Sat.), 112mg Chol., 5g Fiber, 28g Pro., 40g Carb., 934mg Sod.

Kitchen tips

❋ **Add some green.** Stir snipped chives or finely chopped scallions into the crust batter before spreading on top of the chili mixture.

❋ **Turn up the heat.** Toss in a chopped, seeded jalapeño when you cook the onion. Or add a few shakes of hot sauce.

Prep: 20 min.
Cook: 5 hr.
Serves: 8
Cost per serving:
$1.37

- 2 Tbsp. plus ¼ cup vegetable oil
- 1 large onion, chopped
- 2 cloves garlic, minced
- 2 Tbsp. chili powder
- 1½ lb. ground turkey
- 1 28-oz. can crushed tomatoes with liquid
- 1 cup low-sodium beef broth
- 1 15-oz. can kidney beans, drained and rinsed
- ¾ cup all-purpose flour
- ¾ cup yellow cornmeal
- 2 tsp. baking powder
- ½ tsp. salt
- 1 large egg, beaten
- ¾ cup milk
- 1 cup grated Cheddar

1 Mist slow-cooker insert with cooking spray. Warm 2 Tbsp. oil in a large skillet over medium-high heat. Add onion and cook, stirring, until softened, 2 to 3 minutes. Add garlic and chili powder and

Chicken Potpie

Prep: 40 min.
Bake: 25 min.
Serves: 8
Cost per serving:

$1.38

FILLING:
- **2 Tbsp. canola oil**
- **1 onion, chopped**
- **1 rib celery, thinly sliced**
- **½ red bell pepper, seeded and diced**
- **½ cup all-purpose flour**
- **3 cups low-sodium chicken broth**
- **1 cup nonfat milk**
- **1½ lb. boneless, skinless chicken breasts, cut into 1-inch pieces**
- **1 cup frozen peas**
- **2 carrots, diced**
- **Salt and pepper**

TOPPING:
- **2½ cups all-purpose flour**
- **2 tsp. baking powder**
- **½ tsp. salt**
- **3 Tbsp. unsalted butter, cut into small pieces**
- **2 Tbsp. canola oil**
- **1 cup plus 2 Tbsp. nonfat milk**

1 Make filling: Warm oil in a large saucepan over medium-high heat. Add onion, celery and bell pepper; cook, stirring often, until softened, about 7 minutes. Add flour; stir for 1 minute. Add broth and bring to a boil, scraping browned bits from bottom of saucepan. Reduce heat to medium and simmer, stirring, until mixture is thick and creamy.

2 Reduce heat to medium-low and stir in milk. Add chicken and cook, stirring, until firm and opaque, about 7 minutes. Stir in peas and carrots. Season with salt and pepper. Pour into a 2-quart baking dish.

3 Make topping: Preheat oven to 425°F. Pulse flour, baking powder and salt in a food processor. Pulse in butter until mixture resembles coarse meal. With machine on, add oil and 1 cup milk. Process just until a ball forms. Turn out onto floured work surface; knead for 10 seconds. Roll dough to ½-inch thickness. Use a 2-inch cookie cutter to form 16 biscuits. Place biscuits on top of filling; brush with remaining milk.

4 Bake potpie until filling is bubbling and biscuits are lightly browned on top, about 25 minutes. Serve hot.
PER SERVING: 423 Cal., 13g Fat (4g Sat.), 62mg Chol., 3g Fiber, 29g Pro., 46g Carb., 525mg Sod.

Chicken and Red Bean Tostadas

Prep: 20 min.

Bake: 9 min.

Serves: 4

Cost per serving:

$3.27

- 4 10-inch flour tortillas
- 2 Tbsp. vegetable oil
- 3 grilled chicken breast halves, chopped (about 12 oz. total)
- 1 15-oz. can red beans, drained and rinsed
- 1½ cups shredded Monterey Jack
- 4 cups shredded romaine lettuce (from 1 head)
- 1½ cups tomato salsa
- ½ cup low-fat sour cream

1 Arrange racks in top and bottom thirds of oven and preheat to 400°F. Line 2 large, rimmed baking sheets with foil. Place tortillas on baking sheets and brush with oil. Bake until lightly browned, 4 to 5 minutes.

2 Divide chicken, beans and cheese among tortillas and return to oven. Bake tostadas until cheese has melted, 3 to 4 minutes. Remove from oven and top each tostada with ¼ of lettuce, salsa and sour cream. Serve immediately.

PER SERVING: 580 Cal., 30g Fat (14g Sat.), 98mg Chol., 7g Fiber, 38g Pro., 39g Carb., 1,592mg Sod.

Kitchen tips

✳ **Make it healthier.** Are you watching your weight? Use less cheese and try a reduced-fat variety (swapping in 1 cup of reduced-fat shredded Colby-Jack cheese, for example, saves you 85 calories and 8 grams of fat per serving). Add more lettuce and some chopped tomatoes or more salsa to bulk up the dish. Switching to whole-wheat tortillas is another way to boost the fiber and other nutrients.

✳ **Mix beans.** Red beans are pretty in this dish, but you can use any kind you have on hand. Black beans or low-fat refried beans work just as well, or try a colorful mixture. Or spoon warm canned vegetarian chili on top to punch up the flavor. Look for lower-sodium varieties available in the supermarket.

✳ **Go veggie.** To make this dish vegetarian, simply leave out the chicken. Boost it with more beans and some vegetables, such as chopped jicama, shredded carrots and drained canned pickled jalapeños. Add sliced avocado on top.

Chicken Provençal

Chicken Provençal

Prep: 10 min.
Cook: 15 min.
Serves: 4
Cost per serving:

$2.45

- 4 boneless, skinless chicken breast halves, trimmed, pounded to ½-inch thickness
- Salt
- ¼ cup all-purpose flour
- 2 Tbsp. vegetable oil
- 3 cloves garlic, minced
- ½ cup white wine
- 1 15-oz. can diced tomatoes, drained
- ⅓ cup kalamata olives, pitted and chopped
- 1 Tbsp. finely chopped fresh parsley

1 Sprinkle chicken all over with salt. Place flour in a shallow bowl. Dredge chicken in flour on both sides, shaking off excess.

2 Warm oil in a large nonstick skillet over medium-high heat until hot. Sauté chicken until golden and cooked through, turning once, 5 to 7 minutes total. Remove chicken to a plate; tent with foil to keep warm.

3 Add garlic to skillet and sauté until fragrant, about 30 seconds. Stir in wine and tomatoes, scraping up any browned bits from bottom of skillet. Bring to a boil and cook, stirring often, 2 to 3 minutes. Stir in olives.

4 Place chicken on 4 plates; spoon sauce on top. Sprinkle with parsley and serve immediately.
PER SERVING: 370 Cal., 14g Fat (3g Sat.), 106mg Chol., 1g Fiber, 41g Pro., 12g Carb., 948mg Sod.

Pretzel-Crusted Chicken Nuggets

Prep: 15 min.
Bake: 25 min.
Serves: 4
Cost per serving:

$1.79

- 2 cups salted pretzel twists (about 3 oz.)
- ½ cup grated Parmesan
- ½ cup all-purpose flour
- ¼ tsp. pepper
- 2 large eggs
- 1 lb. boneless, skinless chicken breasts, cut into 2-inch pieces

1 Preheat oven to 400°F and coat a large baking sheet with cooking spray. Place pretzels and Parmesan in a food processor and process until coarsely ground and well mixed, 20 to 30 seconds. Transfer to a large bowl.

2 Combine flour and pepper in a separate bowl. Beat eggs with 1 tsp. water in a third bowl.

3 Roll a chicken piece in flour mixture until thoroughly coated. Dip in eggs, allowing excess to drip off. Transfer to pretzel mixture and turn until thoroughly coated. Place chicken on baking sheet. Repeat with remaining pieces of chicken. Bake until lightly browned, 20 to 25 minutes.
PER SERVING: 355 Cal., 8g Fat (3g Sat.), 182mg Chol., 1g Fiber, 37g Pro., 30g Carb., 638mg Sod.

Kitchen tips

❉ **Switch cuts.** Make this recipe with boneless, skinless chicken thighs. Bake for about 10 minutes longer.

❉ **Get saucy.** Serve the nuggets with ponzu, a Japanese dipping sauce made of lemon juice, soy sauce, sugar, vinegar and grated fresh ginger. Or offer a honey-mustard or barbecue option if you prefer.

BEN FINK; FOOD STYLING: STEPHANA BOTTOM

Chicken Tamale Casserole

onion is translucent, about 4 minutes. Add garlic and chili powder and sauté 1 minute.

3 Add chicken and chiles and season with salt and pepper. Raise heat to high. Sauté until chicken is cooked through, about 5 minutes. Pour in enchilada sauce. Bring to a boil. Spoon mixture into baking dish.

4 In a large bowl, combine buttermilk and cornbread. Sprinkle ½ cup cheese over chicken mixture; spread cornbread mixture evenly on top. Sprinkle with remaining cheese. Bake until top is golden, about 20 minutes.

PER SERVING: 262 Cal., 8g Fat (1g Sat.), 84mg Chol., 1g Fiber, 29g Pro., 15g Carb., 590mg Sod.

Kitchen tips

✳ **Add some heat.** If you'd like the dish to be spicier, toss in a chopped, seeded jalapeño when you sauté the onion and bell pepper. Try a spicy enchilada sauce, too.

✳ **Go dark.** Using boneless, skinless chicken thighs instead of breasts will save some money. Or try a combination of both. To save the most, buy a whole chicken.

Prep: 20 min.
Cook: 30 min.
Serves: 8
Cost per serving:

$2.13

- 2 Tbsp. vegetable oil
- 1 medium onion, chopped
- 1 small red bell pepper, seeded and chopped
- 1 clove garlic, minced
- 2 tsp. chili powder
- 2 lb. boneless, skinless chicken breasts, diced
- 1 4-oz. can diced green chiles, drained
- Salt and pepper
- 1 15-oz. can medium red enchilada sauce
- ½ cup buttermilk
- 4 cups crumbled cornbread
- 1½ cups shredded Cheddar

1 Preheat oven to 350°F. Mist a 9-by-13-inch baking dish with cooking spray.

2 Warm oil in a large skillet over medium heat. Add onion and bell pepper; sauté until

Kitchen tips

✳ **Spice it up.** Add ground cumin and turmeric or cayenne to the marinade for a kick.

✳ **Vary the meat.** Re-create this meal another night with beef cubes or shrimp instead of chicken.

✳ **Take it outside.** Try making this dish on your grill. The kebabs will take about 9 minutes to cook.

Yogurt-Marinated Chicken Kebabs

Prep: 10 min.

Soak: 30 min.

Chill: 2 hr.

Cook: 15 min.

Serves: 4

Cost per serving:

$3.46

- 1⅓ cups low-fat plain yogurt
- 2 Tbsp. plus 1 tsp. fresh lemon juice
- 1⅓ tsp. ground coriander
- 3 large cloves garlic, crushed
- Salt and pepper
- 2 lb. boneless, skinless chicken breasts, cut into 1-inch cubes
- 1 large red bell pepper, cored, seeded and cut into 1-inch chunks
- 1 small onion, cut into 1-inch chunks
- 1 Tbsp. olive oil

1 In a large ziplock bag, combine yogurt, lemon juice, coriander and garlic. Season with pepper. Add chicken to bag, seal bag and rub vigorously to coat chicken with marinade. Refrigerate for at least 2 hours or overnight.

2 Soak 8 9-inch wood skewers in water for 30 minutes prior to grilling. Wipe marinade off chicken; discard marinade. Thread chicken cubes onto skewers, alternating with bell pepper and onion. Season with salt.

3 Heat grill pan over medium-high heat, brush with oil, add kebabs (in batches if necessary) and cover with foil. Reduce heat to medium; grill, turning frequently, until chicken is cooked through, about 12 minutes. Serve kebabs with grilled pita bread, rice and a salad or green vegetable.

PER SERVING: 357 Cal., 7g Fat (2g Sat.), 137mg Chol., 2g Fiber, 57g Pro., 14g Carb., 199mg Sod.

Chicken with Lemon and Capers

Prep: 5 min.

Cook: 20 min.

Serves: 4

Cost per serving:

$2.64

- **4 boneless, skinless chicken breast halves (about 5 oz. each)**
- **Salt and pepper**
- **⅓ cup all-purpose flour**

- **3 Tbsp. unsalted butter**
- **3 Tbsp. vegetable oil**
- **¼ cup lemon juice**
- **½ cup white wine**
- **¼ cup capers, rinsed**

1 Preheat oven to 200°F. Sprinkle chicken with salt and pepper; dredge in flour. Warm 1 Tbsp. butter and 2 Tbsp. oil in a large skillet over medium-high heat until butter foams. Add 2 chicken breast halves; cook until browned, about 3 minutes. Flip chicken; cook until firm and browned on other side, about 3 minutes longer. Transfer to a platter and loosely cover with foil.

2 Add 1 Tbsp. each butter and oil to skillet; cook remaining chicken. Add to platter, cover and place in oven.

3 Add lemon juice and wine to skillet; bring to a boil, scraping up browned bits from bottom of pan. Boil, stirring occasionally, until thickened, about 5 minutes. Remove from heat; stir in capers and remaining 1 Tbsp. butter. Cook, stirring, until butter melts. Season with salt and pepper. Pour sauce over chicken and serve.

PER SERVING: 387 Cal., 18g Fat (7g Sat.), 122mg Chol., 1g Fiber, 41g Pro., 10g Carb., 1,010mg Sod.

Chicken and Dumplings

Prep: 20 min.
Cook: 45 min.
Serves: 8
Cost per serving:
$1.81

STEW:
- ½ cup all-purpose flour
- ½ tsp. salt
- ½ tsp. pepper
- ½ tsp. garlic powder
- ½ tsp. onion powder
- 1 tsp. chopped fresh thyme
- 1 tsp. chopped fresh sage
- 2 lb. boneless, skinless chicken thighs, cut into 1-inch pieces
- 2 Tbsp. canola oil
- 2 large carrots, thinly sliced
- 2 ribs celery, thinly sliced
- 2 cups frozen pearl onions, thawed
- 4 cups low-sodium chicken broth
- ½ cup half-and-half
- 1 cup frozen peas

DUMPLINGS:
- 1 cup whole-wheat flour
- ½ cup all-purpose flour
- ½ tsp. baking soda
- ¼ tsp. salt
- 1 Tbsp. chopped fresh thyme
- ¼ tsp. chopped fresh sage
- 1¼ cups buttermilk

1 Make stew: In a large ziplock bag, mix flour, salt, pepper, garlic powder, onion powder, thyme and sage. Add chicken; toss until pieces are coated.

2 Warm 1 Tbsp. oil in a large pot over medium heat. Shake excess flour mixture from chicken (reserve leftover flour), add chicken to pot and cook, stirring, until browned, about 10 minutes. Remove to a plate. Warm remaining oil in pot. Add carrots, celery and onions; sauté 6 minutes. Sprinkle with reserved flour; sauté 2 minutes. Pour in broth; bring to a boil, stirring. Reduce heat to low; simmer 10 minutes, stirring occasionally. Return chicken to pot, stir in half-and-half; simmer 5 minutes.

3 Make dumplings: Combine both flours, baking soda, salt, thyme and sage. Stir in buttermilk just until a sticky dough forms.

4 Stir peas into chicken mixture. Drop in tablespoonfuls of dough and cover; simmer until dumplings are cooked through, about 15 minutes. Serve immediately.
PER SERVING: 367 Cal., 11g Fat (3g Sat.), 102mg Chol., 5g Fiber, 32g Pro., 34g Carb., 500mg Sod.

Bacon-Wrapped Chicken Breasts with Sage

Prep: 10 min.
Cook: 46 min.
Serves: 8
Cost per serving:

$1.29

- 8 boneless, skinless chicken breast halves, trimmed
- Salt
- 16 sage leaves
- 8 slices thick-cut bacon

- 1½ Tbsp. all-purpose flour
- ½ cup low-sodium chicken broth
- ¼ cup fresh lemon juice

1 Preheat oven to 400°F. Lightly mist a 9-by-13-inch baking dish with cooking spray.

2 Sprinkle chicken with salt; place 2 sage leaves on each breast half. Wrap a bacon slice around each chicken piece; place chicken in baking dish. Bake until chicken is cooked through and interior registers 165°F on an instant-read thermometer, about 40 minutes.

3 Transfer chicken to a platter and cover loosely with foil. Skim fat from juices in baking dish and pour them into a small saucepan. Place over medium-high heat; whisk in flour until a paste forms, about 1 minute. Whisk in broth and lemon juice; bring to a boil. Reduce heat to medium and cook, whisking, until sauce is smooth and has thickened, about 2 minutes. Remove from heat. Whisk juices that have accumulated on platter into sauce. Pour sauce on chicken; serve.

PER SERVING: 225 Cal., 7g Fat (2g Sat.), 92mg Chol., 1g Fiber, 37g Pro., 3g Carb., 502mg Sod.

Chicken and Chorizo Paella

Prep: 10 min.
Cook: 20 min.
Serves: 6
Cost per serving:

$2.49

- 1¼ lb. boneless, skinless chicken breasts, cut into 2-inch chunks
- Salt
- ¼ cup all-purpose flour
- 2 Tbsp. vegetable oil
- 1 medium onion, finely chopped
- 2 cloves garlic, finely chopped
- 4 oz. cooked chorizo, cut into ¼-inch-thick rounds
- 1½ cups long-grain rice
- 3½ cups low-sodium chicken broth
- 1 15-oz. can diced tomatoes, drained
- 1 cup frozen peas

1 Lightly sprinkle chicken with salt and dredge in flour on all sides. Warm 1 Tbsp. oil in a large, deep nonstick skillet over medium-high heat. Cook chicken, turning often, until browned on all sides, about 6 minutes total. Transfer to a plate.

2 Warm remaining oil in skillet. Add onion and garlic and cook, stirring often, until softened, about 3 minutes. Add chorizo and cook until lightly browned, about 2 minutes. Stir in rice, broth, tomatoes and ½ tsp. salt. Bring to a boil, add chicken, cover, reduce heat to low and cook until rice is tender and chicken is cooked through, 10 to 12 minutes.

3 Remove from heat, stir in peas, cover and let stand until peas are heated through, about 5 minutes.

PER SERVING: 481 Cal., 14g Fat (4g Sat.), 71mg Chol., 2g Fiber, 36g Pro., 52g Carb., 780mg Sod.

*Bacon-Wrapped
Chicken Breasts with Sage*

Turkey Meatball Subs

Prep: 35 min.
Chill: 30 min.
Cook: 25 min.
Yield: 8 subs
Cost per serving:

$2.34

- 2 large eggs
- ⅓ cup seasoned bread crumbs
- ½ cup finely chopped parsley
- ⅔ cup finely grated Parmesan
- 4 cloves garlic, minced

- 2 lb. lean ground turkey
- 1 24-oz. jar marinara sauce
- 8 crusty sub-style rolls
- 2½ Tbsp. extra-virgin olive oil
- 12 oz. sliced provolone

1 Whisk eggs with 3 Tbsp. water. Stir in bread crumbs and let stand 5 minutes. Add parsley, Parmesan, garlic and turkey; mix gently until well combined. Moisten hands and roll mixture into 24 1½-inch balls. Transfer to a dish large enough to accommodate all meatballs. Refrigerate for 30 minutes.

2 Pour marinara sauce into a wide, deep pot with a lid and warm over medium-high heat. Add meatballs (sauce will not completely cover them), cover and cook 10 minutes. Uncover and turn meatballs. Cover and cook until meatballs are no longer pink inside (cut one to test), about 10 minutes longer.

3 Preheat broiler to high. Cut sub-style rolls lengthwise; drizzle inside of each roll with about 1 tsp. olive oil. Divide cheese among rolls and place rolls on baking sheet. Broil until cheese has melted and bread is lightly toasted, 1 to 2 minutes.

4 Place 3 meatballs on each toasted roll and spoon sauce over; serve.

PER SERVING: 718 Cal., 35g Fat (13g Sat.), 170mg Chol., 2g Fiber, 48g Pro., 54g Carb., 1,407mg Sod.

Chicken, Chile and Cheese Enchiladas

Prep: 45 min.
Bake: 20 min.
Serves: 8
Cost per serving:

$2.44

- 1 Tbsp. vegetable oil
- 1 yellow onion, finely chopped
- 3 cloves garlic, minced
- 1 jalapeño, seeded and minced
- 4 cups cooked, shredded skinless chicken (from a 1½ lb. rotisserie chicken)
- 1 4-oz. can diced mild green chiles, drained
- 2 cups coarsely shredded sharp Cheddar
- 1 16-oz. jar salsa verde
- 1½ cups low-sodium chicken broth
- 16 5½-inch corn tortillas
- ½ cup finely chopped fresh cilantro

1 Preheat oven to 375°F. Mist a 9-by-13-inch baking dish with cooking spray. Warm oil in a medium skillet over medium heat. Add onion and cook, stirring, until softened but not browned, about 5 minutes. Add garlic and jalapeño and cook 2 minutes longer, stirring often. Remove from heat and let cool slightly.

2 In a large bowl, combine onion mixture, chicken, mild green chiles, 1 cup cheese and ½ cup salsa. Stir until well combined.

3 Pour broth into skillet and heat until almost simmering. Working one at a time, dip a corn tortilla into broth, taking care to work quickly so tortilla doesn't become too soft, then transfer to a clean work space. Spoon about 2 Tbsp. of chicken mixture down center of tortilla. Roll tortilla around filling like a cigar and transfer, seam side down, to baking dish. Repeat with remaining tortillas and filling. Pour remaining salsa over top of enchiladas, spreading evenly. Top with remaining cheese.

4 Bake enchiladas, uncovered, until cheese has melted and enchiladas are hot throughout, about 20 minutes. Just before serving, top with cilantro.

PER SERVING: 346 Cal., 14g Fat (6g Sat.), 90mg Chol., 3g Fiber, 32g Pro., 22g Carb., 678mg Sod.

Apricot-Mustard-Glazed Chicken Breasts

Prep: 5 min.
Cook: 1 hr.
Serves: 8
Cost per serving:

$2.50

- 1 cup apricot jam
- ½ cup Dijon mustard
- ½ cup low-sodium chicken broth
- 8 split chicken breast halves, on the bone (about 7 oz. each)
- Salt and pepper
- 2 Tbsp. unsalted butter, cut into pieces and softened
- 12 dried apricots (about 4 oz.), cut into thin slivers

1 Preheat oven to 375°F. In a small saucepan, whisk together jam, mustard and broth. Bring to a boil over high heat, whisking occasionally. Reduce heat to medium-low and cook, stirring, until jam has dissolved, about 3 minutes.

2 Season chicken with salt and pepper. Divide and arrange chicken in a single layer in 2 large baking dishes. Pour jam mixture over chicken and turn to coat. Dot chicken with butter. Scatter apricots over chicken and bake, uncovered, until chicken is lightly browned and cooked through, about 1 hour, turning and basting chicken often during baking time. Let chicken rest for 10 minutes before serving. Serve hot with sauce from baking dishes spooned over top.

PER SERVING: 392 Cal., 5g Fat (3g Sat.), 123mg Chol., 1g Fiber, 47g Pro., 38g Carb., 685mg Sod.

Kitchen tips

❋ **Use other parts.** Make this dish even more economical by cutting up a whole chicken, instead of cooking only breasts. Or use legs and thighs.

❋ **Choose sides.** Serve the chicken with rice, which will help soak up some of the flavorful glaze. A green vegetable or tossed salad helps complete the meal.

CHARLES SCHILLER; FOOD STYLING: LYNN MILLER

Turkey Sloppy Joes

Prep: 12 min.

Cook: 4 hr.

Serves: 6

Cost per serving:

$1.30

- 1 Tbsp. vegetable oil
- 1 large onion, finely chopped
- 2 cloves garlic, finely chopped
- 1½ lb. ground turkey
- 1 tsp. salt
- 1 tsp. chili powder
- 2 tsp. packed light brown sugar
- 1 8-oz. can tomato sauce
- ½ cup ketchup
- ½ tsp. Tabasco
- 6 whole-wheat hamburger buns
- Pickles or pickle relish, optional

1 Warm oil in a large skillet over medium heat. Add onion and garlic and sauté until softened, about 3 minutes. Raise heat to medium-high, stir in turkey, salt and chili powder and cook, stirring to break up meat, until turkey is no longer pink, about 5 minutes.

2 Transfer mixture to slow cooker. Stir in brown sugar, tomato sauce, ketchup, Tabasco and ¼ cup water. Cover and cook on low until bubbling and flavors have developed, 3 to 4 hours. Serve on buns with pickles or pickle relish, if desired.

PER SERVING: 360 Cal., 14g Fat (3g Sat.), 90mg Chol., 3g Fiber, 27g Pro., 31g Carb., 1,133mg Sod.

Kitchen tips

✳ Try it another way. Instead of serving the sloppy joe mixture on buns, toss it with spaghetti or ziti for a new twist.

✳ Sneak in the goods. Even veggie haters aren't likely to notice if you add a couple of finely diced red bell peppers and a shredded carrot when you sauté the onion and garlic.

*Santa Fe
Grilled Chicken
Soft Tacos*

Santa Fe Grilled Chicken Soft Tacos

Prep: 15 min.
Marinate: 30 min.
Cook: 10 min.
Yield: 16 tacos
Cost per serving:

$1.22

- 2 Tbsp. chili powder
- 2 Tbsp. cumin
- 1 Tbsp. paprika
- ½ tsp. crushed red pepper
- ¼ tsp. salt
- ⅛ tsp. pepper
- 1 Tbsp. packed dark brown sugar
- 2 Tbsp. olive oil
- 2½ lb. boneless, skinless chicken breasts, trimmed and pounded thin (about 4 large breasts)
- 16 taco-size soft flour tortillas

1 In a small bowl, combine chili powder, cumin, paprika, red pepper, salt, pepper and brown sugar. Stir in oil; mixture will be moist but crumbly.

2 Rub chicken on all sides with chili mixture. Let stand at room temperature for 30 minutes to marinate (or cover and refrigerate for up to 1 day).

3 Preheat gas grill to medium, or preheat broiler to high and set rack 6 to 8 inches from source of heat. Grill or broil chicken until firm, about 5 minutes per side. Let cool for 5 minutes, then cut into thin strips.

4 Warm tortillas as package label directs. Serve chicken in tortillas.

PER SERVING (1 TACO):
198 Cal., 5g Fat (1g Sat.), 42mg Chol., 2g Fiber, 19g Pro., 17g Carb., 285mg Sod.

Top off your tacos
Take dishes from good to "Wow!" with homemade salsa.

Melon-Pineapple Salsa

Roasted Tomato Salsa

Melon-Pineapple Salsa
Prep: 15 min. **Chill:** 30 min.
Serves: 8 **Cost per serving:** 98¢

- 3 cups diced ripe yet firm cantaloupe, from a 3-lb. melon
- 2 cups diced fresh pineapple, from a 2-lb. pineapple
- 1 red bell pepper, seeded and diced
- ½ red onion, diced
- 1 Tbsp. grated fresh ginger
- 1 small jalapeño, seeded and minced
- 2 Tbsp. lemon or lime juice
- ¼ cup chopped fresh mint leaves
- 2 Tbsp. olive oil
- Salt and pepper

In a large bowl, mix melon, pineapple, bell pepper, onion, ginger, jalapeño and lemon or lime juice. Stir well, cover and chill for at least 30 minutes or up to 6 hours. Just before serving, stir in mint and oil and season with salt and pepper. Serve cold.
PER SERVING: 79 Cal., 4g Fat (1g Sat.), 0mg Chol., 2g Fiber, 1g Pro., 12g Carb., 156mg Sod.

Roasted Tomato Salsa
Prep: 15 min. **Cook:** 20 min.
Serves: 8 **Cost per serving:** 87¢

- 8 to 10 medium plum tomatoes, about 2 lb., halved lengthwise
- 1 red bell pepper, quartered and seeded
- 2 medium jalapeños, halved lengthwise and seeded
- ½ small onion, chopped
- 2 cloves garlic, chopped
- Salt and pepper
- 1 tsp. cumin
- ½ cup packed fresh cilantro

1 Preheat broiler to high; set a rack 4 inches from heat source. Arrange tomatoes cut side down on a broiling pan. Broil, watching carefully and turning pan, until tomatoes are charred, about 10 minutes. Transfer to a plate and let cool.

2 Place bell pepper and jalapeños on broiling pan; broil until blackened and charred, 7 to 10 minutes. Remove to a bowl, cover tightly with plastic wrap and set aside for 10 minutes. Peel pepper and jalapeños, but leave blackened skins on tomatoes. Coarsely chop vegetables.

3 Working in batches if necessary, combine cooked tomatoes, bell pepper and jalapeños with onion, garlic, ½ tsp. salt and ¼ tsp. pepper in a food processor. Pulse briefly until coarsely chopped. (Do not overprocess. The salsa should be chunky.) Pulse in cumin and cilantro. Season with additional salt and pepper. Cover and refrigerate until ready to serve.
PER SERVING: 30 Cal., 0g Fat (0g Sat.), 0mg Chol., 2g Fiber, 1g Pro., 6g Carb., 153mg Sod.

Shredded-Beef Tacos

Beef

Steak Salad

2 Sprinkle steak with salt and pepper, place on baking sheet and broil, turning once, 7 to 10 minutes total for medium-rare. Tent with foil and let rest 5 minutes.

3 Put lettuce and tomatoes in a large bowl. Make dressing: Whisk together all ingredients. Pour on salad; toss to coat.

4 Arrange salad on 6 plates. Thinly slice steak and place on top of salad. Serve with toasted bread.

PER SERVING: 306 Cal., 15g Fat (6g Sat.), 52mg Chol., 2g Fiber, 23g Pro., 18g Carb., 652mg Sod.

Kitchen tips

✳ **Swap dressings.** If a creamy dressing doesn't appeal to you, whip up a quick vinaigrette with red wine vinegar, orange or lemon juice, honey and olive oil.

✳ **Cut up.** Instead of making toast, cut the bread into cubes, toss with olive oil and dried herbs, season with salt and pepper and bake. Add the croutons to the salad just before serving.

Prep: 10 min.
Cook: 15 min.
Serves: 6
Cost per serving:

$2.45

SALAD:
- 1 loaf Italian bread, cut into 12 slices
- 1 clove garlic
- 1 lb. skirt or flank steak
- Salt and pepper
- 1 1-lb. bag romaine hearts, torn
- 12 cherry tomatoes, halved

DRESSING:
- ¼ cup sour cream
- ¼ cup mayonnaise
- 2 tsp. lemon juice
- 1 tsp. mustard
- 1 clove garlic, chopped
- 1 Tbsp. finely chopped fresh parsley
- ¼ tsp. salt

1 Preheat broiler to high; place a rack 5 inches from heat. Line a baking sheet with foil. Place bread slices on baking sheet and toast, turning once, until golden, 2 to 4 minutes total. Rub 1 side of each slice with garlic.

Kitchen tips

✳ Serve with extras.
Offer small bowls
of shredded lettuce,
salsa, sour cream,
guacamole, shredded
Cheddar, pickled
jalapeños and other
taco toppings. A few
lime wedges make a
pretty garnish and give
the tacos extra zing.

✳ Add some heat.
For spicier beef, leave
some of the seeds in
the chipotle. The more
seeds you leave in, the
spicier the beef will be.

Shredded-Beef Tacos

Prep: 10 min.
Cook: 6 hr.
Yield: 12 tacos
Cost per serving:

$1.86

- 1 tsp. salt
- 2 tsp. chili powder
- 1 tsp. cumin
- ½ tsp. coriander
- 2 lb. top round roast
- 1 Tbsp. olive oil
- 1 8-oz. can tomato sauce
- ½ chipotle chile in adobo sauce, seeded and finely chopped
- 4 cloves garlic, finely chopped
- 12 corn tortillas

1 Combine salt, chili powder, cumin and coriander; rub over roast. Warm oil in a pot over medium-high heat. Sear meat on both sides, about 4 minutes total.

2 Place roast in slow cooker. In a bowl, mix tomato sauce, chipotle and garlic; pour on meat. Cover and cook on low until fork-tender, about 6 hours. Shred meat; mix with enough sauce to moisten. Serve in tortillas.

PER SERVING (2 TACOS):
341 Cal., 9g Fat (2g Sat.),
70mg Chol., 4g Fiber, 39g Pro.,
25g Carb., 738mg Sod.

Cola-Braised Brisket

Prep: 15 min.

Cook: 8 hr.

Serves: 10

Cost per serving:

$2.47

- 2 Tbsp. packed light brown sugar
- 1 Tbsp. salt
- 1 Tbsp. sweet paprika
- 2 tsp. onion powder
- 1 tsp. pepper
- 1 4-lb. beef brisket, trimmed
- 2 Tbsp. vegetable oil
- 4 onions, thinly sliced
- 2 cups cola
- 1 28-oz. can crushed tomatoes

1 In a small bowl, combine sugar, salt, paprika, onion powder and pepper and mix well. Rub mixture thoroughly all over brisket. Warm oil in a large pot or Dutch oven over medium-high heat. Cook brisket until browned on all sides, turning with tongs, about 7 minutes total. Carefully transfer meat to slow cooker.

2 Arrange onions on top of brisket. Whisk together cola and tomatoes in a large bowl and pour into slow cooker. Cover and cook on low until meat is fork-tender, 7 to 8 hours.

3 Transfer meat to a cutting board and allow to stand for 10 minutes. Transfer gravy from slow cooker to a bowl or gravy boat. Slice meat against the grain and serve with gravy on the side.

PER SERVING: 321 Cal., 10g Fat (3g Sat.), 69mg Chol., 2g Fiber, 41g Pro., 18g Carb., 1,068mg Sod.

Mediterranean Stuffed Peppers

Prep: 20 min.
Cook: 1 hr.
Serves: 4
Cost per serving:

97¢

- Salt
- ⅓ cup couscous
- 2 tsp. cumin
- 1½ tsp. cinnamon
- ½ tsp. sugar
- 2 tsp. vegetable oil
- 2 cloves garlic, minced
- 8 oz. ground beef
- 1 medium onion, chopped
- 2 tsp. grated fresh ginger
- 1 8-oz. can tomato sauce
- 1 15-oz. can chickpeas, drained and rinsed
- 8 dried apricots, chopped into ¼-inch dice
- 4 green bell peppers (about 6½ oz. each), tops sliced off, seeded and cored

1 Bring ½ cup lightly salted water to a boil. Stir in couscous. Cover, remove from heat and let stand until water has absorbed, about 5 minutes. Fluff couscous lightly with a fork and re-cover. In a small bowl, combine cumin, cinnamon, sugar and ½ tsp. salt.

2 Warm oil in a large skillet over medium-high heat. Add garlic and sauté until golden, about 1 minute. Add beef and cook, stirring and breaking it up, until no longer pink, about 4 minutes. Add onion and ginger; cook, stirring, until onion begins to soften, about 4 minutes longer. Sprinkle cumin mixture over beef and sauté for 1 minute.

3 Reduce heat to medium-low and stir in tomato sauce, ½ cup water, chickpeas and apricots. Stir well, scraping up browned bits from bottom of skillet. Remove from heat and stir in couscous.

4 Preheat oven to 375°F and mist an 8-inch baking dish with cooking spray. If peppers don't stand upright, cut a tiny slice off bottom of each pepper to level. Stuff peppers with meat mixture and place them in baking dish. Pour ¼ cup water into baking dish, cover with foil and bake until peppers are tender when pierced with a knife, about 45 minutes.

PER SERVING: 343 Cal., 10g Fat (3g Sat.), 37mg Chol., 8g Fiber, 20g Pro., 44g Carb., 890mg Sod.

Kitchen tip

✳ **Use a different fruit.** If you don't like dried apricots or don't have them in your pantry, feel free to swap in ⅓ cup golden raisins. If the raisins are dry, soak them in hot water before using.

Korean Beef Stir-Fry

Prep: 5 min.
Cook: 6 min.
Serves: 4
Cost per serving:

$2.27

- 2 Tbsp. soy sauce
- 2 Tbsp. rice wine or dry white wine
- 1 tsp. Asian sesame oil
- 3 cloves garlic, finely chopped
- 1 lb. flank steak, sliced thin against the grain
- 1 Tbsp. vegetable oil
- 4 scallions, white and light green parts, finely chopped
- 1 Tbsp. sesame seeds

1 Whisk soy sauce, wine, sesame oil and garlic in a large bowl. Add flank steak and toss to coat. Let stand about 10 minutes.

2 In a nonstick skillet or wok over high heat, warm oil until hot. Add flank steak; cook, stirring often, until meat is no longer pink, 2 to 3 minutes. Add scallions and sesame seeds and stir-fry for 1 minute longer; serve.
PER SERVING: 242 Cal., 13g Fat (3g Sat.), 48mg Chol., 1g Fiber, 26g Pro., 4g Carb., 331mg Sod.

Kitchen tips

❋ **Chill out.** To get the thinnest slices, wrap the flank steak well and place it in the freezer for 30 minutes before slicing. Be sure your knife is sharp.

❋ **Pick sides.** Serve the beef with rice and sautéed snow peas.

Beef Chili Bake

Prep: 15 min.
Cook: 45 min.
Serves: 4
Cost per serving:

98¢

- 2 tsp. vegetable oil
- 3 cloves garlic, minced
- 8 oz. ground beef
- 1 medium onion, chopped
- 2 Tbsp. chili powder
- 1 tsp. cumin
- 1 tsp. salt
- ⅛ tsp. cayenne, optional
- 1 Tbsp. all-purpose flour
- 1 14.5-oz can diced tomatoes
- 1 15.5-oz. can red kidney beans
- 1 8.5-oz. box corn muffin mix
- 2 scallions, white and light green parts, thinly sliced

1 Preheat oven to 400°F. Warm oil in a skillet over medium-high heat. Sauté garlic 1 minute. Add beef; cook, stirring and breaking it up, until no longer pink, about 4 minutes. Add onion; sauté until softened, about 5 minutes.

2 Stir chili powder, cumin, salt and cayenne, if desired, into beef mixture; sauté 1 minute. Add flour and cook, stirring, for 1 minute. Stir in tomatoes with liquid and ¼ cup of water, then stir in beans with liquid. Cook, stirring, until thickened, about 2 minutes. Transfer mixture to an 8-inch baking dish.

3 Prepare muffin mix as label directs. Fold in scallions. Spread batter on beef mixture. Bake until top is golden, 20 to 25 minutes.
PER SERVING: 463 Cal., 15g Fat (4g Sat.), 74mg Chol., 9g Fiber, 25g Pro., 59g Carb., 1,751mg Sod.

Kitchen tip

❋ **Make it a meal.** Toss a quick salad to go with this rich dish.

Korean Beef Stir-Fry

Kitchen tips

✻ **Top it off.** For a quick glaze, spread more tomato sauce on top of the meat loaf before baking. Or slather on the traditional ketchup.

✻ **Bump up the nutrition.** To make this tasty meat loaf healthier, substitute brown rice for the white. Brown is higher in fiber, magnesium and other nutrients.

Italian-Style Meat Loaf

Prep: 10 min.
Cook: 1 hr. 15 min.
Serves: 6
Cost per serving:

$1.01

- 1 lb. ground chuck
- 1 small onion, finely chopped
- 2 cloves garlic, finely chopped
- 1 cup tomato sauce
- ¼ cup finely chopped fresh parsley
- 1 large egg
- 1 tsp. salt
- ¼ tsp. fennel seeds
- 1 cup cooked white rice

1 Preheat oven to 350°F. Line a baking sheet with heavy-duty aluminum foil.

2 In a large bowl, combine ground chuck, onion, garlic, tomato sauce, parsley, egg, salt, fennel seeds and rice. Mix with your fingers until well combined (but do not overmix).

3 Pat mixture into an 8-by-4-inch loaf and place on baking sheet. Bake until an instant-read thermometer inserted into center registers 160°F and meat is no longer pink, about 1 hour and 15 minutes. Let stand 10 minutes before slicing.

PER SERVING: 229 Cal., 12g Fat (5g Sat.), 87mg Chol., 1g Fiber, 17g Pro., 12g Carb., 665mg Sod.

Southwestern Hamburgers

2 Sprinkle beef with chili powder and 1 tsp. salt. Mix gently with your hands to distribute seasonings. Shape into 4 patties. Broil hamburgers until they reach desired doneness, turning once, about 8 minutes total for medium-rare. Serve hamburgers on buns with guacamole on top. **PER SERVING:** 551 Cal., 27g Fat (8g Sat.), 102mg Chol., 6g Fiber, 37g Pro., 42g Carb., 753mg Sod.

Kitchen tips

✳ **Go all out.** Offer a few additional accompaniments to give these burgers more Southwestern flair, such as Jack cheese, sliced tomatoes and diced pickled jalapeños.

✳ **Wrap it up.** For a Mexican spin, cook the ground beef in a skillet instead of forming it into patties. Make burritos by wrapping the beef in warmed whole-wheat tortillas with the guacamole and some rice, beans, cheese and salsa.

Prep: 5 min.
Cook: 8 min.
Serves: 4
Cost per serving:

$1.75

- 1 ripe avocado, peeled, pitted and coarsely chopped
- 1 Tbsp. finely chopped shallot
- 1 Tbsp. lime juice
- ¼ tsp. crushed red pepper
- 1½ tsp. salt
- 1 lb. ground chuck
- 1 tsp. chili powder
- 4 whole-wheat hamburger buns

1 Preheat broiler to high and place a rack about 8 inches from heat source. Combine avocado, shallot, lime juice, crushed red pepper and ½ tsp. salt in a bowl. Lightly mash avocado with back of a fork to break up chunks. Cover with plastic wrap, pressing directly onto surface of guacamole, and chill until ready to serve.

Beef and Vegetable Stew

Prep: 20 min.
Cook: 8 hr. 10 min.
Serves: 8
Cost per serving:

99¢

- **¼ cup all-purpose flour**
- **Salt and pepper**
- **1½ lb. beef stew meat, cut into 1-inch pieces**
- **2 Tbsp. vegetable oil**
- **2 carrots, cut into 1-inch slices**
- **2 parsnips, cut into 1-inch slices**
- **1 medium turnip, peeled, cut into 1-inch pieces**
- **1 large sweet potato, peeled, cut into 1-inch pieces**
- **¼ cup pearl barley**
- **1 large onion, chopped**
- **2 cloves garlic, minced**
- **1 cup thinly sliced celery**
- **1 14-oz. can low-sodium beef broth**
- **1 Tbsp. Worcestershire sauce**
- **2 Tbsp. tomato paste**
- **1 bay leaf**
- **1 tsp. dried thyme**

1 Combine flour and 1 tsp. each salt and pepper in a large ziplock bag. Add beef, seal bag and toss to coat.

2 Warm 1 Tbsp. oil in a large skillet over medium-high heat. Remove beef pieces from bag, shaking to remove excess flour (reserve flour). Cook beef, stirring, until meat is brown on all sides, about 5 minutes. Work in batches, if necessary. Remove meat to slow cooker and top with carrots, parsnips, turnip, sweet potato and barley.

3 Add remaining 1 Tbsp. oil to skillet and cook onion, garlic and celery for 3 minutes, stirring often. Sprinkle with reserved flour; cook, stirring, for 1 minute. Add broth, 3 cups water, Worcestershire, tomato paste, bay leaf, thyme and 1 tsp. each salt and pepper; bring to a boil, scraping up browned bits on bottom of skillet. Pour mixture on top of meat and vegetables in slow cooker, stir, cover and cook on low until meat and vegetables are tender, 7 to 8 hours. Season with salt and pepper, if desired.

PER SERVING: 274 Cal., 13g Fat (4g Sat.), 56mg Chol., 4g Fiber, 19g Pro., 20g Carb., 374mg Sod.

Meatball Calzones

Prep: 20 min.
Cook: 22 min.
Serves: 4
Cost per serving:

$3.50

- **1 cup part-skim ricotta**
- **1 cup shredded reduced-fat mozzarella**
- **1 10-oz. package frozen chopped spinach, thawed and squeezed dry**
- **1 lb. frozen pizza dough, thawed**
- **1½ cups tomato sauce**
- **1 12-oz. package frozen cooked meatballs, each cut in half**

1 Preheat oven to 425°F. Mist a large, rimmed baking sheet with nonstick cooking spray. Combine ricotta, mozzarella and spinach in a bowl.

2 Divide dough into four equal pieces and roll each piece into an 8-inch circle. Spoon 2 Tbsp. sauce in center of each dough round and spread over dough, leaving a 1-inch border. Divide cheese mixture among dough rounds. Top each dough round with meatball halves.

3 Fold dough over filling to create half-moon shapes. Press edges to seal calzones. Bake until golden, 18 to 22 minutes. Serve with remaining sauce for dipping.

PER SERVING: 662 Cal., 22g Fat (9g Sat.), 79mg Chol., 4g Fiber, 43g Pro., 69g Carb., 1,805mg Sod.

Kitchen tips

❋ **Save some dough.** Instead of buying the frozen variety at the grocery store, ask the proprietors of your favorite pizzeria if they sell their dough. It's often less expensive and typically is fresher than what's available at supermarkets. Use what you need; freeze the rest.

❋ **Balance it out.** This is a rich, hearty main dish. To make it a more well-rounded meal, offer a green vegetable on the side, such as sautéed string beans or steamed broccoli, or toss a simple salad.

❋ **Lighten up.** To cut calories and fat, look for frozen turkey meatballs or vegetarian ones.

Bolognese Sauce

Bolognese Sauce

Prep: 30 min.
Cook: 8 hr. 30 min.
Serves: 8
Cost per serving:

$1.55

- **1 Tbsp. unsalted butter**
- **1 small onion, chopped**
- **1 rib celery, finely chopped**
- **1 carrot, finely chopped**
- **2 lb. lean ground beef**
- **Salt and pepper**
- **Pinch of nutmeg**
- **1 cup whole milk**
- **1 cup white wine**
- **2 28-oz. cans crushed tomatoes**

1 Melt butter in a large saucepan over medium heat. Add onion, celery and carrot and cook, stirring, until vegetables have softened, about 5 minutes. Increase heat to high, add beef and cook, breaking up with a spoon, until meat is no longer pink, about 5 minutes. Season with salt, pepper and nutmeg.

2 Pour milk and wine into saucepan and bring to a boil. Reduce heat to medium-low and cook at a lively simmer until most of liquid has evaporated, about 15 minutes.

3 Transfer mixture to slow cooker, stir in tomatoes, cover and cook on low for 8 hours. Remove cover, stir and continue to cook until sauce is slightly thickened, about 30 minutes longer. Serve hot, over pasta, if desired.

PER SERVING: 313 Cal., 14g Fat (6g Sat.), 82mg Chol., 4g Fiber, 27g Pro., 16g Carb., 822mg Sod.

Mustard-Glazed Beef Skewers

Prep: 10 min.
Cook: 10 min.
Serves: 4
Cost per serving:

$2.42

- **½ cup olive oil**
- **2 Tbsp. Dijon mustard**
- **2 Tbsp. chopped fresh thyme or 1 tsp. dried**
- **16 (1½-inch) cubes of beef (about 12 oz.)**
- **2 red or yellow bell peppers, cut into 1-inch squares**
- **1 large red onion, cut into 12 wedges**
- **Salt and pepper**

1 Preheat broiler and set oven rack about 6 inches from heat source. Line a broiler pan with heavy-duty aluminum foil or a double layer of regular-strength foil.

2 In a small bowl, mix together olive oil, mustard and thyme. Thread alternating cubes of beef, pieces of bell pepper and wedges of onion onto 4 skewers. Brush each skewer with oil-mustard mixture. Season with salt and pepper.

3 Broil skewers, turning once, until beef is no longer pink outside and onions are slightly charred, about 10 minutes. Serve with broiled tomato halves and herbed rice, if desired.

PER SERVING: 412 Cal., 35g Fat (7g Sat.), 43mg Chol., 2g Fiber, 18g Pro., 7g Carb., 245mg Sod.

Kitchen tips

✳ Pick the beef. Choose flank steak, round or chuck for the cubes—any of these cuts will work well for this recipe. Or, for a Mediterranean touch, use lamb stew meat.

✳ Get a jump on prep. You can make the sauce and assemble the skewers up to a day in advance. Cover and chill. Bring the meat to room temperature before cooking.

Eye of Round Roast with Pan Juices

4 Place roasting pan on stove over medium-high heat. Pour in wine; cook, stirring to pick up any browned bits on bottom of pan, until liquid has reduced slightly, about 3 minutes. Pour in broth, increase heat to high and boil until thickened and syrupy, about 5 minutes.

5 Slice roast against grain into ¼-inch-thick slices. Arrange meat on a platter and spoon some juices on top. Serve additional juices on the side.

PER SERVING: 261 Cal., 6g Fat (2g Sat.), 71mg Chol., 0g Fiber, 45g Pro., 1g Carb., 324mg Sod.

Kitchen tips

❋ **Cook to the right doneness.** Eye of round is a lean cut of beef, so take care not to overcook the meat or it will be tough.

❋ **Add trimmings.** This dish is great with roasted vegetables or potatoes on the side. Place the meat on a platter and garnish it with some of the vegetables and a few sprigs of fresh herbs.

Prep: 10 min.
Cook: 1 hr. 13 min.
Serves: 8
Cost per serving:

$2.48

- 1 eye of round roast, about 3½ lb., trimmed
- Salt and pepper
- 2 tsp. olive oil
- ½ cup dry red wine
- 1 cup low-sodium beef broth

1 Preheat oven to 425°F. Season meat all over with salt and pepper.

2 Oil a roasting rack and place it in a roasting pan that's just large enough to hold the beef.

3 Warm oil in a skillet over medium-high heat. Add beef and cook, turning often, until lightly browned all over, 5 to 10 minutes. Transfer beef to rack and roast until a meat thermometer inserted into thickest part reads 125°F for medium-rare, 50 to 55 minutes. Remove roast to a cutting board, tent with foil and let rest 10 minutes.

Kitchen tips

✳ **Chill out.** Freeze extra portions of soup in single-serving containers for busy weeknights.

✳ **Change the vegetables.** Swap parsnips for the carrots, if you prefer. Toss in 1 or 2 chopped ribs of celery when you sauté the onions.

Beef and Barley Soup

Prep: 15 min.
Cook: 7 hr.
Serves: 8
Cost per serving:

$2.56

- 2 Tbsp. vegetable oil
- 2 onions, chopped
- 10 oz. white button mushrooms, sliced
- 2 lb. lean beef stew meat, cut into ½-inch pieces
- 6 cups canned low-sodium beef broth
- 2 carrots, chopped
- 1 28-oz. can diced tomatoes with juice
- 1 Tbsp. Worcestershire sauce
- 1 tsp. dried thyme
- ½ tsp. garlic powder
- ⅔ cup pearl barley
- Salt and pepper

1 Warm 1 Tbsp. vegetable oil in a large skillet over medium-high heat. Add onions and mushrooms and cook, stirring frequently, until vegetables have softened slightly and mushrooms have released their water, about 7 minutes. Scrape vegetables into slow cooker. Warm remaining 1 Tbsp. vegetable oil in same skillet. Add beef and cook, stirring, until meat is browned on all sides, about 5 minutes (if skillet is too small, cook beef in batches, adding more oil if needed). Scrape beef into slow cooker.

2 Pour 1 cup broth into skillet and stir with a wooden spoon to scrape up any browned bits on bottom of pan. Pour broth from skillet into slow cooker. Add remaining broth, carrots, tomatoes, Worcestershire sauce, thyme, garlic powder, barley and 1 tsp. salt. Stir, cover and cook on low until meat is tender, 6 to 7 hours. Season with salt and pepper and serve hot.
PER SERVING: 448 Cal., 28g Fat (10g Sat.), 82mg Chol., 4g Fiber, 26g Pro., 24g Carb., 899mg Sod.

Ground Sirloin with Mushroom Cream Sauce

Prep: 5 min.

Cook: 25 min.

Serves: 4

Cost per serving:

$2.63

- 1½ lb. ground sirloin
- Salt and pepper
- 2 Tbsp. vegetable oil
- 1 small onion, diced
- 10 oz. mushrooms, sliced (about 4 cups)
- ½ cup heavy cream
- 2 Tbsp. chopped fresh parsley

1 Thoroughly mix sirloin, 1 tsp. salt and 1 tsp. pepper. Form 4 patties, each about 4 inches wide.

2 Warm oil in a large skillet over medium-high heat. Cook patties until browned, about 5 minutes per side. Transfer to a plate; cover with foil to keep warm.

3 Pour off all but 1 Tbsp. fat from skillet. Add onion; cook, stirring, until softened, about 2 minutes. Add mushrooms and cook, stirring, until they have given off their liquid and are soft, about 10 minutes. Stir in cream and cook until slightly thickened, about 2 minutes. Stir in parsley, season with salt and pepper. Return patties to skillet. Turn patties a few times over low heat until they're coated in sauce and warmed through, about 3 minutes. Spoon mushrooms on top, then serve right away.

PER SERVING: 420 Cal., 27g Fat (11g Sat.), 145mg Chol., 1g Fiber, 39g Pro., 5g Carb., 1,012mg Sod.

Kitchen tips

❋ **Don't mind the many mushrooms.** They'll cook down when they release their liquid in the skillet.

❋ **Choose sides.** Serve the patties with a scoop of mashed potatoes or some rice to soak up the sauce. A green vegetable such as steamed broccoli or a simple tossed salad rounds out the meal.

Smoky Chipotle Meat Loaf

Prep: 15 min.
Bake: 55 min.
Serves: 8
Cost per serving:

$1.18

- ⅓ cup barbecue sauce
- 2 canned chipotle chiles, seeded
- 1 Tbsp. adobo sauce (from canned chiles)
- 2 large eggs
- 1 Tbsp. Worcestershire sauce
- ½ tsp. salt
- ¼ tsp. pepper
- 2 cloves garlic, minced
- 1 small onion, finely minced
- 1½ lb. lean ground beef
- 1 cup quick-cooking oats
- 3 Tbsp. ketchup

1 Preheat oven to 350°F. Mist a 9-by-5-inch loaf pan with cooking spray.

2 Combine barbecue sauce, chipotles, adobo sauce, eggs, Worcestershire sauce, salt and pepper in a food processor and process until smooth. Transfer to a large bowl and add garlic, onion, beef and oats. Mix gently but thoroughly with your hands. Lightly pack mixture into loaf pan.

3 Bake for 45 minutes. Carefully spread ketchup on top; bake for 10 minutes longer, or until an instant-read thermometer inserted into center reaches 160°F. Let stand 5 to 10 minutes; serve.

PER SERVING: 300 Cal., 16g Fat (6g Sat.), 104mg Chol., 3g Fiber, 21g Pro., 18g Carb., 354mg Sod.

Kitchen tips

✳ **Make it unplugged.** If you don't have a food processor, whisk the first 7 ingredients together vigorously. Be sure to finely chop the chipotles.

✳ **Enjoy leftovers.** Turn extra meat loaf into a hearty lunch by making it into sandwiches. Put slices on whole-grain bread or rolls.

Shepherd's Pie

Prep: 30 min.
Cook: 1 hr.
Serves: 6
Cost per serving:

96¢

- 2½ lb. baking potatoes, peeled, cut into 2-inch pieces
- Salt and pepper
- ¾ cup low-fat milk
- 2 Tbsp. low-fat sour cream
- 8 oz. extra-lean ground beef
- 1 large onion, finely diced
- 1 rib celery, finely diced

- 1 carrot, finely diced
- 1 cup mushrooms, finely diced
- 4 cloves garlic, minced
- 2 Tbsp. all-purpose flour
- 2 cups low-sodium beef broth
- 1 Tbsp. Worcestershire sauce
- ½ cup cooked lentils
- 1 cup frozen peas, thawed

1 Place potatoes in a pot, cover with cold, salted water, bring to a boil over medium-high heat and cook until potatoes are tender, about 20 minutes. Drain, transfer potatoes to a large bowl and mash with milk and sour cream. Season with salt and pepper.

2 Warm a large nonstick skillet over medium heat until hot. Add beef and cook, breaking up with a spoon, until no longer pink, about 5 minutes. Add onion, celery, carrot and mushrooms; sauté for 8 minutes. Add garlic and sauté 2 minutes longer. Sprinkle flour on top and cook, stirring, for 2 minutes. Stir in broth, Worcestershire and lentils; bring to a boil, reduce heat to low and simmer for 10 minutes.

3 Preheat oven to 375°F. Mist a 9-by-13-inch baking dish with cooking spray. Stir peas into meat mixture and season with salt and pepper. Spoon meat mixture into baking dish and carefully spread mashed potatoes on top. Bake for 30 minutes. If potatoes are not brown enough, turn broiler on high and broil until potatoes are golden, about 2 minutes, watching carefully to avoid burning.
PER SERVING: 297 Cal., 4g Fat (2g Sat.), 28mg Chol., 6g Fiber, 18g Pro., 50g Carb., 459mg Sod.

Beef up your meals for less

Shop smart, store well and cook right, and you can enjoy meat without busting your budget.

▶ **Buy in bulk.** Purchase several family-size packages of ground beef at a time, especially if they're on sale. Divide the meat into ½- or 1-lb. portions, wrap tightly and freeze. If you find steaks on sale, cut them into cubes or strips for stir-fries, then wrap and freeze.

Bonus tip To make weeknight meals even quicker, take one or two of those 1-lb. portions of ground beef and cook them. Let cool, then wrap and freeze. All you will have to do is defrost to make quick tacos, pasta sauce or sloppy joes. (Label each portion with the date and amount.)

▶ **Plan for sales.** Meat often goes on sale just after a big holiday, like Christmas, Easter or July Fourth. You can get great bargains on roasts, ham or hot dogs and fill up your freezer.

▶ **Try something new.** If you see an inexpensive cut in your grocery store's meat case that doesn't look familiar, ask the butcher to recommend the best way to prepare it. You can get a great deal and add a new recipe to your repertoire.

▶ **Stretch out.** Instead of going all meat, mix beans, oats or rice into recipes for burgers or meat loaf (see Smoky Chipotle Meat Loaf on previous page, which uses quick-cooking oats). Not only is it cost-effective, it also adds nutrients and fiber (people won't taste the difference).

Shepherd's Pie

*Pork Tenderloin
with Sweet and Sour Cabbage*

Pork

Dijon-Marmalade-Glazed Baked Ham

Cover pan and ham with more heavy-duty aluminum foil. Bake ham for 1½ hours.

3 Make glaze: Melt orange marmalade in small saucepan over medium heat, stirring occasionally. Whisk in Dijon mustard and 2 Tbsp. water. Bring mixture to a boil; cook until glaze thickens, about 10 minutes. Set glaze aside.

4 Remove ham from oven and raise oven temperature to 425°F. Remove aluminum foil covering ham and brush warm glaze all over ham. Return ham to oven and bake uncovered until glaze caramelizes, about 30 minutes. Remove ham from oven, tent loosely with aluminum foil to keep warm and let stand 30 minutes before serving.

PER SERVING: 491 Cal., 16g Fat (5g Sat.), 142mg Chol., 0g Fiber, 61g Pro., 23g Carb., 889mg Sod.

Prep: 15 min.
Bake: 2 hr.
Stand: 30 min.
Serves: 10
Cost per serving:

$2.74

- 1 8-lb. bone-in baked ham
- 30 whole cloves
- 1 12-oz. jar orange marmalade
- ¼ cup Dijon mustard

1 Preheat oven to 350°F. Line a large baking pan with heavy-duty aluminum foil. Place ham cut side down in center of pan.

2 Trim any rind or excess fat from ham with a sharp knife; score outside of ham with sharp knife in a decorative diamond pattern (as shown) and insert a whole clove into each diamond point.

Kitchen tip

❋ **Dress up your platter.** Fresh herbs make a nice garnish for the ham. Thyme, rosemary and chives all look pretty—especially if they're flowering.

Kitchen tip

* **Make room.** If you can't fit the noodles in the skillet along with the pork mixture, remove the meat and vegetables to a large bowl with tongs or a slotted spoon. Add the noodles to the skillet with the sauce. Toss for 1 minute, then add to the bowl and toss again.

Pork Lo Mein

Prep: 15 min.

Cook: 20 min.

Serves: 6

Cost per serving:

$1.75

- 12 oz. soba noodles or whole-wheat spaghetti
- ¼ cup reduced-sodium soy sauce
- 1 Tbsp. plus 1 tsp. cornstarch
- 2 tsp. sugar
- 2 Tbsp. rice vinegar
- 1 cup low-sodium chicken broth
- 2 lean, boneless center-cut pork chops (about 12 oz. total), cut into thin strips
- 2 tsp. canola oil
- 4 cups thinly sliced cabbage (from about ½ head)
- 1 medium carrot, grated
- 1 cup snow peas, halved crosswise (about 3 oz.)
- Salt and pepper
- 2 scallions, thinly sliced

1 Bring a large pot of water to boil. Cook soba noodles until tender, about 5 minutes, or as package label directs (spaghetti will take longer, about 10 minutes). Drain.

2 In a large bowl, whisk together soy sauce, cornstarch, sugar, vinegar and broth. Add pork and toss to coat. Set aside to marinate for 10 minutes at room temperature.

3 Warm oil in a large nonstick wok or skillet over medium-high heat. Add pork and marinade; stir-fry until meat is no longer pink, about 3 minutes. Add cabbage and stir-fry until just wilted, about 2 minutes. Stir in carrot and snow peas; cook, stirring vigorously, until snow peas are slightly softened yet firm, about 2 minutes. Stir in noodles and toss to coat with sauce and warm through, about 1 minute. Season with salt and pepper. Divide mixture among 6 bowls, sprinkle with scallions and serve.

PER SERVING: 315 Cal., 3g Fat (1g Sat.), 31mg Chol., 6g Fiber, 23g Pro., 51g Carb., 1,210mg Sod.

Baked Pasta with Peas, Cheese and Ham

Prep: 15 min.

Cook: 30 min.

Serves: 6

Cost per serving:

$1.52

- Salt
- 12 oz. penne or farfalle
- 4 Tbsp. unsalted butter

- ¼ cup all-purpose flour
- 1 tsp. dry mustard
- 2 cups milk
- 1 cup half-and-half
- 12 oz. mild low-fat Cheddar, shredded (about 3 cups)
- 1½ cups frozen peas
- 3 oz. diced smoked ham (about ¾ cup)
- 1½ cups crushed saltines (about 25)

1 Preheat oven to 400°F. Bring a pot of salted water to boil. Add pasta and cook until just tender, about 8 minutes. Drain and set aside.

2 Melt 3 Tbsp. butter in a large ovenproof skillet over medium heat. Whisk in flour, mustard and ½ tsp. salt. Slowly whisk in milk and half-and-half and bring to a simmer. Stir in cheese, a little at a time, until melted. Remove pan from heat and stir in peas, ham and pasta. Stir to coat with sauce.

3 Sprinkle crumbs over pasta; dot with remaining 1 Tbsp. butter. Bake until bubbling, about 20 minutes.

PER SERVING: 613 Cal., 23g Fat (12g Sat.), 63mg Chol., 5g Fiber, 32g Pro., 72g Carb., 955mg Sod.

Grilled Pork Tenderloin
with Green Tomato–Pineapple Salsa

Prep: 20 min.
Cook: 45 min.
Serves: 8
Cost per serving:

$2.05

- 4 medium green tomatoes (about 1 lb.), cored and chopped
- 1 small onion, chopped
- 1 Tbsp. lemon juice
- 2 Tbsp. olive oil
- ½ fresh pineapple, cored, cut into ¼-inch dice (about 2 cups)
- 2 1½-lb. whole pork tenderloins
- 2 cloves garlic, thinly sliced
- Salt and pepper

1 Combine tomatoes, onion, lemon juice and olive oil in a large bowl. Stir in pineapple, cover and chill until ready to serve. (Salsa can be made up to 1 day ahead. Keep covered and refrigerated.) Makes about 4 cups.

2 Preheat a gas grill to medium-low. Make small incisions all over tenderloins with a sharp paring knife and insert slices of garlic until meat is well studded. Season tenderloins with salt and pepper. Oil grates and grill pork, turning often, until a meat thermometer inserted at thickest part of tenderloins reaches 160°F and tenderloins are lightly browned on outside and show no pink color inside, about 45 minutes. Remove tenderloins to a cutting board and let rest about 10 minutes.

3 Season green tomato–pineapple salsa with salt and pepper. Serve cold with thin slices of pork.

PER SERVING: 241 Cal., 6g Fat (2g Sat.), 111mg Chol., 2g Fiber, 37g Pro., 9g Carb., 234mg Sod.

Kitchen tip

✳ **See red.** Can't find green tomatoes at your supermarket? Swap in red ones, or try yellow or orange if they're available.

Potato, Pepper and Chorizo Hash with Fried Eggs

Prep: 15 min.
Cook: 35 min.
Serves: 4
Cost per serving:

$1.31

- 2 8-oz. baking potatoes, cut into ½-inch dice
- Salt
- 1 Tbsp. vegetable oil
- 1 onion, thinly sliced
- 1 red bell pepper, seeded, cut into ½-inch dice
- 4 oz. chorizo, thinly sliced
- 4 large eggs
- 1 Tbsp. finely chopped cilantro

1 Place potatoes in a pot, cover with 1 inch of water, stir in ½ tsp. salt and bring to a boil. Reduce heat and simmer until tender, 5 to 7 minutes. Drain.

2 Warm oil in a 10-inch ovenproof nonstick skillet over medium-high heat. Add onion and cook, stirring often, until tender, about 3 minutes. Add bell pepper and chorizo and cook, stirring often, until pepper has softened, 3 to 5 minutes. Stir in potatoes, season with salt and cook, stirring occasionally, until potatoes begin to brown, about 5 minutes.

3 Press lightly on mixture so it forms a cake. Reduce heat to medium and continue to cook until golden and crisp on bottom, 5 to 7 minutes.

4 Preheat broiler to high. Carefully break eggs onto potato cake. Place pan under broiler and cook until whites are set, about 2 minutes. Sprinkle with cilantro and serve.

PER SERVING: 363 Cal., 20g Fat (6g Sat.), 237mg Chol., 4g Fiber, 17g Pro., 30g Carb., 721mg Sod.

Red-Currant-Pomegranate-Glazed Ham

Prep: 5 min.
Cook: 6 hr. 30 min.
Stand: 15 min.
Serves: 12
Cost per serving:

$1.47

- 1 small bone-in half ham (about 6 lb.)
- 1 cup pomegranate juice
- ½ cup red currant jelly
- 2 Tbsp. Dijon mustard
- ¼ cup packed dark brown sugar

1 Place ham in slow cooker, pour in pomegranate juice, cover and cook on low until completely warmed through, 4 to 6 hours, basting once or twice. Put jelly in a small saucepan over medium-low heat and cook, stirring, until softened. Pour jelly through a fine-mesh sieve into a bowl, discarding solids. Cover and refrigerate jelly until ready to use.

2 In a small pan, combine 3 Tbsp. cooking liquid from slow cooker with jelly, mustard and sugar. Bring to a boil over high heat, stirring until sugar has dissolved. Remove 1 cup cooking liquid from slow cooker; discard. Pour jelly mixture on top of ham. Cover slow cooker; increase heat to high. Cook for about 30 minutes, basting often, until shiny and glazed. Transfer ham to a platter and let stand for 15 minutes; serve.

PER SERVING: 373 Cal., 12g Fat (4g Sat.), 138mg Chol., 0g Fiber, 48g Pro., 16g Carb., 221mg Sod.

*Potato, Pepper
and Chorizo Hash
with Fried Eggs*

Pork and Beans

Prep: 20 min.
Cook: 5 hr. 15 min.
Serves: 8
Cost per serving:

$2.84

- **2 onions, thinly sliced**
- **2 strips bacon, chopped**

- **1 3-lb. boneless whole pork loin roast**
- **1½ cups barbecue sauce**
- **2 Tbsp. packed light brown sugar**
- **1 tsp. garlic powder**
- **2 15-oz. cans red kidney beans, drained and rinsed**
- **Salt, optional**

1 Scatter onions and bacon evenly over bottom of slow cooker. Place pork roast on top (cut roast in half or in thirds if it won't fit in your slow cooker in one piece). In a small bowl, whisk together barbecue sauce, brown sugar and garlic powder. Pour sauce mixture evenly over pork. Cover slow cooker and cook on low until meat is tender, about 5 hours.

2 Remove roast from slow cooker and shred meat. Return shredded meat to slow cooker, stir in beans, cover and cook until heated through, about 15 minutes. Season with salt, if desired, and serve right away.

PER SERVING: 431 Cal., 17g Fat (6g Sat.), 113mg Chol., 6g Fiber, 40g Pro., 27g Carb., 884mg Sod.

Honey-Mustard Pork Skewers

Set aside at room temperature.

2 Preheat broiler to high and line a broiling pan with foil. (Alternatively, preheat a gas grill to medium.) Divide peppers and pork into 8 portions; thread onto skewers, alternating (begin and end with pepper; use about 6 pepper pieces and 5 pork cubes per skewer). Thread each skewer as close as possible to center of pieces, to facilitate turning. Season with salt and pepper.

3 Broil or grill 6 to 8 inches from heat source, turning often, until slightly browned and pork is cooked through, 12 to 15 minutes.

PER SERVING: 148 Cal., 5g Fat (1g Sat.), 55mg Chol., 1g Fiber, 18g Pro., 8g Carb., 369mg Sod.

Soak: 30 min.
Prep: 5 min.
Cook: 15 min.
Serves: 8
Cost per serving:
$1.62

- ¼ cup Dijon mustard
- 2 Tbsp. honey
- 1 Tbsp. olive oil
- 1 pork tenderloin (about 1½ lb.), halved lengthwise, cut into 1-inch cubes
- 2 bell peppers, cored, seeded, cut into 1-inch squares
- Salt and pepper

1 Soak 8 bamboo skewers in cold water for 30 minutes. Stir mustard, honey and oil in a large bowl until smooth. Add pork cubes and toss to coat.

Kitchen tip

✳ **Use another cut.** Pork shoulder is less expensive than tenderloin, and it makes great skewers. Wrap and refrigerate or freeze extra meat.

Pork Tenderloin with Cornmeal-Herb Crust

Prep: 5 min.
Cook: 20 min.
Serves: 4
Cost per serving:

$2.21

- ¼ cup yellow cornmeal
- 1 cup fresh parsley, finely chopped
- ½ cup fresh sage, finely chopped
- 2 cloves garlic, finely chopped
- 2 Tbsp. olive oil
- 1 tsp. salt
- 1 1¼-lb. pork tenderloin

1 Preheat oven to 500°F. Line a baking sheet with heavy-duty aluminum foil. Mist foil with cooking spray or brush with vegetable oil.

2 In a medium bowl, combine cornmeal, parsley, sage, garlic, oil and salt; stir until well mixed. Pat tenderloin dry. Using your fingers, press cornmeal mixture onto tenderloin, coating it completely. Transfer to prepared baking sheet and roast for 10 minutes. Using tongs, carefully turn tenderloin over; roast until an instant-read thermometer inserted into thickest part of meat registers 145°F, 8 to 10 minutes longer.

3 Remove tenderloin to a cutting board.

Tent meat loosely with foil and let stand for 10 minutes. Slice pork and serve.

PER SERVING: 286 Cal., 12g Fat (3g Sat.), 92mg Chol., 3g Fiber, 31g Pro., 11g Carb., 661mg Sod.

Kitchen tips

✳ **Select sides.** Serve this pork with rice or baked potatoes. Round out the meal with green beans, steamed broccoli or a leafy salad.

✳ **Switch seasonings.** Fresh herbs are best in this dish, but if you prefer to use dried, swap in about 2½ tablespoons sage and 5 tablespoons parsley.

✳ **Give it a break.** Allowing the pork to rest before slicing it lets the juices in the meat redistribute, so you end up with better texture and flavor.

Orecchiette with Broccoli, Tomatoes and Sausage

Prep: 10 min.
Cook: 25 min.
Serves: 6
Cost per serving:

$1.21

- 1 Tbsp. olive oil
- 2 cloves garlic, finely chopped
- 8 oz. hot or sweet Italian sausage, removed from casings
- 1 15-oz. can diced tomatoes, with juice
- Salt
- 1 lb. orecchiette or pasta shells
- 4 cups small broccoli florets (from 1 head)
- Shredded Parmesan, optional

1 Warm oil in a medium skillet over medium-high heat. Add garlic and sauté until fragrant, about 30 seconds. Add sausage and cook, breaking up with a wooden spoon, until meat loses its pink color, about 6 minutes. Add tomatoes with their juice and ¼ tsp. salt and cook, stirring occasionally, until most of juice has evaporated and sauce has thickened, about 10 minutes.

2 While sauce is cooking, bring a large pot of salted water to boil. Stir in pasta; cook according to package label directions. In last 2 minutes of cooking time, stir in broccoli and continue to cook until pasta is al dente and broccoli is tender. Drain, return to pot and toss with sauce. Serve immediately, with shredded Parmesan on the side, if desired.

PER SERVING: 471 Cal., 15g Fat (4g Sat.), 29mg Chol., 4g Fiber, 18g Pro., 66g Carb., 799mg Sod.

Kitchen tips

✳ **Try another pasta.**
Orecchiette ("little ears" in Italian) works well in this dish, but you can substitute penne, if you prefer. Swap in whole-wheat pasta for added nutrients.

✳ **Make it spicier.**
To give this dish a touch more heat, use hot sausage and add a few pinches of crushed red pepper when you cook the tomatoes.

*Chinese
Roast Pork*

Chinese Roast Pork

Prep: 10 min.
Cook: 6 hr. 15 min.
Serves: 8
Cost per serving:

$2.36

- 1 3-lb. boneless pork loin
- Salt and pepper
- 2 Tbsp. vegetable oil
- 1 onion, chopped
- 1 3-inch piece fresh ginger, peeled and chopped
- 2 cloves garlic, minced
- ½ cup low-sodium soy sauce
- 2 Tbsp. packed dark brown sugar
- 2 tsp. Chinese five-spice powder

1 Trim pork of excess fat and season with salt and pepper. Warm oil in a large skillet over medium-high heat. Add pork and brown on all sides, 5 to 7 minutes.

2 Transfer pork to slow cooker. Pour off all but 1 Tbsp. fat from skillet. Add onion, ginger and garlic to skillet and cook, stirring, until softened, about 3 minutes. Add soy sauce, brown sugar and five-spice powder. Cook, stirring, until sugar has dissolved, about 1 minute. Pour over pork.

3 Cover and cook on low until meat is very tender when pierced with a knife, about 6 hours. Remove pork to a cutting board, tent with foil and let stand 10 minutes. Thinly slice and serve.

PER SERVING: 252 Cal., 8g Fat (2g Sat.), 111mg Chol., 1g Fiber, 37g Pro., 7g Carb., 832mg Sod.

Kitchen tip

✳ **Wrap it up.** Be sure your pork loin is tied tightly (you can ask your butcher to do it). Otherwise it might be difficult to slice.

Stuffed Twice-Baked Sweet Potatoes

Prep: 15 min.
Cook: 35 min.
Serves: 4
Cost per serving:

$2.02

- 4 sweet potatoes (8 to 10 oz. each)
- 4 strips bacon
- ¾ cup sour cream
- ¼ cup sun-dried tomatoes packed in oil, drained, patted dry and finely chopped
- 2 scallions, white and light green parts, chopped
- ½ tsp. salt
- 6 oz. shredded Cheddar

1 Pierce potatoes all over with a fork and place in a shallow microwave-safe baking dish. Microwave on high, turning every 2 minutes, until tender, about 10 minutes total. Set aside to cool for 10 minutes.

2 In a skillet over medium-high heat, cook bacon until crisp, turning once, about 8 minutes total. Move bacon to a paper towel–lined plate to cool. Crumble bacon.

3 Preheat oven to 400°F. Halve potatoes lengthwise. Scoop out flesh into a large bowl, leaving shells of about ¼-inch thickness. Place shells, cut sides up, on a baking

sheet; bake until crisp, about 5 minutes.

4 Stir bacon, sour cream, tomatoes, scallions, salt and half of cheese into bowl with potato flesh. Divide filling among potato shells, sprinkle with remaining cheese and return to oven. Bake until cheese is bubbling, about 10 minutes.

PER SERVING: 564 Cal., 28g Fat (15g Sat.), 91mg Chol., 8g Fiber, 21g Pro., 58g Carb., 1,097mg Sod.

Pork Tenderloin with Sweet and Sour Cabbage

skillet and sauté until tender, about 3 minutes. Add cabbage, vinegar and sugar and cook, stirring often, until cabbage has wilted, about 5 minutes.

4 Place tenderloin on top of cabbage and roast until a meat thermometer inserted into center registers 150°F, about 15 minutes. Let stand 5 minutes. Slice pork; serve with cabbage.

PER SERVING: 346 Cal., 14g Fat (3g Sat.), 81mg Chol., 3g Fiber, 28g Pro., 27g Carb., 630mg Sod.

Kitchen tips

✳ **Get prepped.** Before you begin cooking, check the pork. If there's a silver membrane on it, slice it off and discard.

✳ **Round out the meal.** Serve this healthful dish with a green vegetable, like sautéed broccoli, or roasted red potatoes.

✳ **Change colors.** Use a green cabbage instead of red, if you prefer.

Prep: 15 min.
Cook: 30 min.
Serves: 4
Cost per serving:

$2.35

- 1 1-lb. pork tenderloin
- ½ tsp. salt
- 2 Tbsp. vegetable oil

- 2 Tbsp. whole-grain mustard
- 2 slices bacon, chopped
- 1 onion, thinly sliced
- ½ large head red cabbage, cored and thinly sliced
- ¼ cup cider vinegar
- ¼ cup sugar

1 Preheat oven to 450°F. Sprinkle pork with salt.

2 Warm oil in a large ovenproof skillet over medium-high heat. Add pork; brown on all sides, turning occasionally. Transfer to a plate; let cool slightly. Spread mustard on pork.

3 Add bacon to skillet and cook, stirring occasionally, until it begins to crisp, about 1 minute. Add onion to

Kitchen tips

✳ **Take shape.** You can make these little patties into larger disks, if you prefer. They may need a few extra minutes to cook.

✳ **Make wraps.** Serve the pork and greens with grilled flatbreads, if you like, so everyone can create their own wraps. Offer chopped tomatoes and red onions on the side.

Grilled Spiced Pork Patties with Greens

Prep: 10 min.
Cook: 10 min.
Serves: 4
Cost per serving:

$1.89

- 1 lb. ground pork
- 1 tsp. ground coriander
- 1 tsp. cumin
- ½ tsp. cinnamon
- ¼ tsp. nutmeg
- 1 large egg, beaten
- ½ onion, finely chopped
- ¼ cup finely chopped fresh parsley
- 2 cloves garlic, chopped
- 1½ tsp. salt
- 1 cup plain whole-milk yogurt
- 1½ tsp. lemon juice
- 10 cups mixed salad greens

1 Preheat gas grill to medium. In a large bowl, combine pork, coriander, cumin, cinnamon, nutmeg, egg, onion, parsley, 1 clove garlic and 1 tsp. salt. Mix thoroughly with your hands. Form mixture into 1½-inch balls, then press into football shapes.

2 Oil grill grates. Grill patties, turning once, until cooked through, 8 to 10 minutes total.

3 In a small bowl, whisk together yogurt, lemon juice and remaining garlic and salt. Divide salad greens among 4 serving plates. Place grilled patties on top of greens and drizzle with yogurt sauce. Serve immediately.

PER SERVING: 390 Cal., 27g Fat (11g Sat.), 142mg Chol., 2g Fiber, 26g Pro., 11g Carb., 419mg Sod.

Thai Pork with Red Curry

Prep: 15 min.

Cook: 5 hr. 18 min.

Serves: 6

Cost per serving:

$2.08

- 1¼ cups low-sodium chicken broth
- 1 14-oz. can reduced-fat coconut milk
- 1 onion, thickly sliced
- 1 red bell pepper, cored and sliced lengthwise
- 1 8-oz. package white mushrooms, quartered
- 2 Tbsp. red curry paste
- 3 Tbsp. vegetable oil
- 2½ lb. boneless pork butt or shoulder, cubed
- 1½ tsp. salt
- ½ tsp. black pepper
- 1 cup chopped cilantro

1 Mix ¾ cup chicken broth, coconut milk, onion, bell pepper, mushrooms and curry paste in a slow cooker. Stir to combine.

2 Warm 1 Tbsp. oil in a skillet over medium-high heat. Season pork cubes with salt and pepper and add a third of pork to skillet. Brown meat for 6 minutes. Transfer pork to slow cooker. Repeat with remaining 2 batches of pork and 2 Tbsp. oil.

3 Pour remaining ½ cup chicken broth into skillet, scraping up any browned bits from bottom of pan; add to slow cooker and stir. Cover and cook on high heat for 5 hours. Using a slotted spoon, skim grease off top prior to serving.

4 Sprinkle cilantro on stew. Serve over rice, if desired.

PER SERVING: 450 Cal., 28g Fat (10g Sat.), 129mg Chol., 2g Fiber, 40g Pro., 8g Carb., 1,370mg Sod.

Barbecued-Pork Sliders

Prep: 20 min.
Chill: 8 hr.
Cook: 5 hr. 45 min.
Yield: 24
Cost per serving:

$2.57

- 1 4-lb. pork shoulder roast
- 24 small dinner rolls

SPICE RUB:
- 1 Tbsp. paprika
- 1 Tbsp. garlic powder
- 1 Tbsp. packed dark brown sugar
- 1 Tbsp. dry mustard
- 1 Tbsp. onion powder
- 1 tsp. dried thyme
- 1 tsp. dried oregano
- Salt and pepper
- ½ tsp. cayenne pepper

SAUCE:
- 2 onions, chopped
- 1 green bell pepper, seeded and chopped
- ½ cup packed dark brown sugar
- ¼ cup cider vinegar
- 1 6-oz. can tomato paste
- 1½ Tbsp. chili powder
- 1 tsp. dried mustard
- 1 Tbsp. Worcestershire sauce
- 1 tsp. salt

PICKLED ONION:
- 1 Tbsp. sugar
- 1 tsp. salt
- ½ cup white vinegar
- 1 red onion, thinly sliced

1 Remove skin and excess fat from pork roast. Make spice rub: Combine all ingredients in a bowl and rub all over meat. Place pork on a large plate, cover with plastic wrap and refrigerate for 8 hours or overnight.

2 Make sauce: Stir together all ingredients in slow cooker, place pork on top, cover and cook on high until meat is tender and can be shredded easily with a fork, about 5½ hours.

3 Make pickled onion: Stir sugar and salt into white vinegar until dissolved; stir in onion. Cover and refrigerate for 2 to 3 hours, stirring occasionally.

4 Remove pork from slow cooker; let cool slightly. Remove 2 cups of sauce. Shred meat. Stir pork back into slow cooker, cover and cook for 15 minutes.

5 Split dinner rolls, top with meat and pickled onion. Serve, passing reserved sauce separately.

PER SERVING (3 SLIDERS):
612 Cal., 18g Fat (6g Sat.), 88mg Chol., 5g Fiber, 53g Pro., 58g Carb., 3,252mg Sod.

Sautéed Pork Chops with Pineapple and Mint

Prep: 15 min.
Cook: 15 min.
Serves: 4
Cost per serving:

$2.44

- 4 6-oz. boneless pork chops, trimmed, pounded to ¾-inch thickness
- Salt
- 1 Tbsp. vegetable oil
- 1½ cups pineapple chunks, diced
- 1 Tbsp. finely chopped fresh mint
- ½ tsp. crushed red pepper

1 Sprinkle pork chops on both sides with salt. Warm oil in a large skillet over medium-high heat. Add chops and sear on one side until well browned, 3 to 4 minutes. Reduce heat to medium, turn chops and continue to cook until an instant-read thermometer inserted into center of chops reads 140°F to 145°F, 4 to 6 minutes longer. Transfer to a platter and cover with foil to keep warm.

2 Add pineapple and 2 Tbsp. water to skillet. Cook, stirring to scrape up any browned bits on bottom of skillet, until warmed through, about 2 minutes. Stir in mint and crushed red pepper. Spoon over chops and serve.

PER SERVING: 341 Cal., 20g Fat (6g Sat.), 87mg Chol., 1g Fiber, 32g Pro., 9g Carb., 927mg Sod.

Kitchen tip

✱ **Open a can.** Fresh pineapple is more flavorful, but if it isn't available in your grocery store, you can use canned to make this dish.

Creamy Pasta Shells with Broccoli and Ham

Prep: 5 min.
Cook: 12 min.
Serves: 4
Cost per serving:

$1.95

- Salt and pepper
- 1 lb. small pasta shells
- 4 cups small broccoli florets (from 1 medium head broccoli)
- 2 Tbsp. unsalted butter
- 1 small onion, finely chopped
- 4 oz. ham, chopped
- ¾ cup heavy cream, warmed

- ½ cup grated Parmesan

1 Bring a large pot of salted water to boil. Add pasta and cook until al dente, 8 to 10 minutes. Add broccoli for last 2 to 3 minutes of cooking time. Drain and return to pot.

2 While pasta is cooking, melt butter over medium heat in a large skillet. Add onion and sauté until softened, about 3 minutes. Add ham and cook, stirring, for 2 minutes longer. Stir in cream, bring to a simmer and cook, stirring occasionally, until thickened, 3 to 5 minutes.

3 Scrape cream mixture into pot with pasta. Toss in cheese. Season with salt and pepper; serve, passing more Parmesan, if desired.

PER SERVING: 819 Cal., 36g Fat (19g Sat.), 107mg Chol., 5g Fiber, 27g Pro., 97g Carb., 849mg Sod.

Sautéed Pork Chops with Pineapple and Mint

Cheddar, Ham and Spinach Strata

Prep: 20 min.
Chill: 6 hr.
Cook: 1 hr.
Serves: 8
Cost per serving:

$2.02

- 3 Tbsp. unsalted butter
- 1 onion, finely chopped
- 1 10-oz. package frozen spinach, thawed, squeezed dry and chopped
- 1½ tsp. salt
- 6 oz. ham, chopped
- 12 oz. grated low-fat Cheddar (about 3 cups)
- 1 large Italian or French bread (about 1 lb.), cut into ½-inch-thick slices
- 10 large eggs
- 1 Tbsp. Dijon mustard
- 3 cups half-and-half

1 Melt butter in a large skillet over medium heat. Add onion and cook, stirring, until softened, about 3 minutes. Stir in spinach and ½ tsp. salt and heat through. Stir in ham. Remove from heat and let cool.

2 Set aside 1 cup cheese, cover and refrigerate. Grease a 9-by-13-inch baking dish; cover bottom of dish with a layer of bread. Cover bread with half of spinach mixture, then half of remaining cheese. Repeat with remaining bread, spinach and cheese.

3 Whisk together eggs, mustard, half-and-half and remaining salt in a bowl. Pour over strata. Press down with a spatula. Cover and refrigerate at least 6 hours or overnight.

4 Uncover strata and bring to room temperature. Preheat oven to 350°F. Sprinkle with reserved cheese and bake until set in center, 50 to 60 minutes. Let stand 5 minutes before serving.

PER SERVING: 516 Cal., 27g Fat (14g Sat.), 331mg Chol., 3g Fiber, 31g Pro., 38g Carb., 1,416mg Sod.

Spicy Asian Pork Tenderloin

knife to slice tenderloin.
Serve warm.

PER SERVING: 229 Cal.,
7g Fat (2g Sat.), 93mg Chol.,
1g Fiber, 30g Pro., 9g Carb.,
629mg Sod.

Kitchen tips

✳ **Choose sides.**
To complete the meal,
serve this tenderloin
with rice and sautéed
snow peas or broccoli
drizzled with just a
little sesame oil and
sprinkled with sesame
seeds. To achieve a
nutrient boost, opt for
brown rice.

✳ **Get saucy.** Look for
hoisin and chili-garlic
sauces in the Asian
foods section of your
grocery store. Can't
find hoisin sauce?
Substitute apple butter.

✳ **Tame the heat.**
If you love Asian
flavors but not the
spiciness, leave out
the chili-garlic sauce.
Instead, stir a finely
minced garlic clove
into the marinade
for a slight bite.

✳ **Use a different
meat.** Pork tenderloin
is delicious and lean,
but you also can make
this dish with chicken.

Prep: 5 min.
Cook: 15 min.
Serves: 4
Cost per serving:

$2.15

- ¼ cup hoisin sauce
- 2 Tbsp. chili-garlic sauce
- 1 tsp. sesame oil
- 1½ Tbsp. rice vinegar
- 1 1¼-lb. pork tenderloin, patted dry

1 Preheat a gas grill
to medium-high. In
a small bowl, combine
hoisin sauce, chili-garlic
sauce, sesame oil and
rice vinegar.

2 Brush pork all over
with sauce. Oil grill
and place pork on
grill grates. Cover and
grill, turning several
times with tongs,
until an instant-read
thermometer inserted
into thickest part
registers 150°F, 12 to
15 minutes total.
Transfer pork to
a plate, tent with foil
and let rest at least
5 minutes. Use a sharp

KANA OKADA; FOOD STYLING: SUSAN VAJARANANT

*Swiss Chard
and Ham Frittata*

Swiss Chard and Ham Frittata

Prep: 10 min.
Cook: 25 min.
Serves: 8
Cost per serving:

70¢

- 2 Tbsp. olive oil
- 2 cloves garlic, chopped
- 1 large bunch Swiss chard (about 12 oz.), tough part of stems removed, leaves sliced
- 1 cup diced ham (about 4 oz.)
- 12 large eggs
- ½ tsp. salt
- ¼ tsp. pepper
- 2 Tbsp. grated Parmesan

1 Preheat oven to 400°F. Warm oil in a large nonstick, ovenproof skillet over medium-high heat. Sauté garlic until fragrant, about 30 seconds. Stir in chard. Cover and cook, stirring twice, until chard is tender, about 5 minutes. Remove cover; stir in ham.

2 Crack eggs into a large bowl, season with salt and pepper and whisk to blend. Pour eggs into skillet over chard and ham. Stir to distribute ingredients as evenly as possible before eggs begin to set.

3 Cook on top of stove, carefully lifting sides of frittata with a spatula to let uncooked eggs flow underneath, until lightly browned around edges, 3 to 5 minutes. Sprinkle frittata with Parmesan, transfer skillet to oven and bake, uncovered, until firm in center and slightly browned on top, about 10 minutes. Cut into wedges; serve.

PER SERVING: 170 Cal., 12g Fat (3g Sat.), 325mg Chol., 1g Fiber, 13g Pro., 3g Carb., 550mg Sod.

BLT Salad

Prep: 15 min.
Cook: 15 min.
Serves: 4
Cost per serving:

$1.95

- 3 cups cubed country bread (¾-inch cubes)
- 2 Tbsp. olive oil
- Salt
- 3 large eggs
- 8 slices bacon
- ¼ cup reduced-fat mayonnaise
- 1 Tbsp. lemon juice
- 1 head iceberg lettuce, shredded
- 1 beefsteak tomato, cut into wedges

1 Preheat oven to 350°F. Toss bread cubes with olive oil and salt on a large, rimmed baking sheet. Bake until golden and crisp, stirring occasionally, about 15 minutes. Let cool completely.

2 Place eggs in a saucepan and cover with cold water. Bring water to a boil over medium-high heat. When water reaches a boil, remove saucepan from heat, cover and let stand for 12 minutes. Drain, run eggs under cold water until cool enough to handle, then peel and quarter.

3 Cook bacon in a large skillet over medium heat until crisp, turning once with tongs, about 12 minutes total. Remove to a paper towel–lined plate to drain and cool. When bacon is cool enough to handle, crumble.

4 In a large bowl, whisk together mayonnaise and lemon juice. Add shredded lettuce and toss to coat. Divide among 4 plates. Arrange tomato wedges, bacon, eggs and croutons on top of lettuce. Serve salad immediately.

PER SERVING: 414 Cal., 26g Fat (7g Sat.), 189mg Chol., 4g Fiber, 18g Pro., 28g Carb., 1,214mg Sod.

*Grilled Shrimp with
Lime-Cilantro Dipping Sauce*

Fish

Curried Tuna Wraps

burrito. Repeat with remaining tortillas, lettuce and tuna. Cut each wrap crosswise on diagonal and serve.

PER SERVING: 293 Cal., 15g Fat (1g Sat.), 47mg Chol., 7g Fiber, 33g Pro., 39g Carb., 1,458mg Sod.

Kitchen tips

✳ **Choose sides.** Serve spoonfuls of mango chutney with the wraps for a sweet, spicy kick. Baked potato chips and a pickle offer a nice crunch.

✳ **Add color.** The whole-wheat tortillas deliver a nutty taste along with fiber and other nutrients. You also can try spinach or tomato tortillas, which provide a shot of color and flavor.

✳ **Unwrap it.** Instead of wraps, try this tuna salad on toasted whole-grain bread or scooped into pitas. Another option: Spoon it on top of mixed greens tossed with a lemon vinaigrette.

✳ **Swap fruits.** Don't have currants? Stir in raisins instead.

Prep: 10 min.

Serves: 4

Cost per serving:

$2.00

- 3 5-oz. cans tuna in water, drained
- ¼ cup slivered almonds, lightly toasted
- 2 Tbsp. minced red onion
- 2 Tbsp. dried currants
- 1 Tbsp. jarred hoisin sauce
- 2 tsp. mild curry powder
- ¼ cup reduced-fat mayonnaise
- Salt and pepper
- 4 romaine lettuce leaves
- 4 whole-wheat tortillas

1 In a bowl, combine tuna, almonds, onion, currants, hoisin sauce, curry powder and mayonnaise ; mix well to combine, breaking up any large chunks of tuna with a fork. Season with salt and pepper.

2 Lay 1 leaf of lettuce in center of a tortilla and top with ¼ of tuna mixture. Fold in edges of tortilla and roll like a

Tilapia Piccata

Prep: 5 min.

Cook: 15 min.

Serves: 4

Cost per serving:

$3.30

- **4 tilapia fillets (about 6 oz. each)**
- **Salt**
- **¼ cup all-purpose flour**

- **2 Tbsp. olive oil**
- **3 Tbsp. unsalted butter**
- **½ cup white wine**
- **¼ cup lemon juice**
- **1 Tbsp. capers**
- **2 Tbsp. finely chopped fresh parsley**

1 Sprinkle fish lightly with salt and dredge in flour on both sides to coat. Warm 1 Tbsp. each olive oil and butter in a skillet over medium-high heat until butter melts. Sauté 2 fillets, turning once, until browned on both sides and cooked through, 3 to 4 minutes total. Transfer fish to a plate; cover with foil. Repeat with another 1 Tbsp. each oil and butter and remaining fish.

2 Pour white wine and lemon juice into skillet and bring to a boil. Remove skillet from heat and stir in capers, parsley and remaining 1 Tbsp. butter. Keep stirring sauce until butter melts. Place each fillet on a plate, pour sauce over fish and serve immediately.

PER SERVING: 414 Cal., 21g Fat (8g Sat.), 133mg Chol., 0g Fiber, 43g Pro., 8g Carb., 479mg Sod.

Grilled Shrimp with Lime-Cilantro Dipping Sauce

Prep: 10 min.
Cook: 6 min.
Serves: 8
Cost per serving:

$3.21

DIPPING SAUCE:
- ½ cup soy sauce
- 2 Tbsp. chopped cilantro
- 2 Tbsp. lime juice
- 1 Tbsp. vegetable oil
- ¼ tsp. sugar

SHRIMP:
- **32 medium to large shrimp (about 2 lb.), peeled and deveined**
- **2 Tbsp. lemon juice**
- **1 Tbsp. grated lemon zest**
- **¼ cup olive oil**
- **2 cloves garlic, minced**
- **Salt and pepper**

1 Preheat broiler or preheat grill to medium-high.

2 Make dipping sauce: Combine soy sauce, cilantro, lime juice, vegetable oil, sugar and 1 Tbsp. water in a small bowl. Mix until sugar dissolves completely. Cover and set aside. (Sauce can be prepared up to 2 days in advance. Bring sauce to room temperature before serving.)

3 Make shrimp: Rinse shrimp under cold running water, drain and pat dry. Place shrimp in a large bowl and add lemon juice and zest, oil and garlic. Season with salt and pepper. Mix well to coat. Thread shrimp flat (through tail and head) on 8 long metal skewers. Cook shrimp about 6 inches from heat until bright pink and firm, about 3 minutes per side. Remove shrimp from skewers to a serving platter and serve warm with dipping sauce on the side.

PER SERVING: 208 Cal., 11g Fat (1g Sat.), 171mg Chol., 0g Fiber, 24g Pro., 3g Carb., 1,218mg Sod.

Salmon Cakes

Prep: 25 min.

Chill: 30 min.

Cook: 20 min.

Serves: 6

Cost per serving:

95¢

- 3 lb. baking potatoes, peeled, cut into 1-inch pieces
- Salt and pepper
- 2 Tbsp. unsalted butter
- 1 14.75-oz. can pink salmon, drained, skin and bones removed, fish flaked
- 1 tsp. dried dill
- 1 Tbsp. chopped fresh parsley
- 2 scallions, white and light green parts, finely chopped
- 2 large eggs
- ½ cup all-purpose flour
- 1 cup plain dry bread crumbs
- 2 Tbsp. vegetable oil

1 Place potatoes into a pot, cover with water and add 1 tsp. salt. Bring to a boil over high heat, reduce heat to medium-low and simmer until potatoes are tender, about 15 minutes. Drain and mash potatoes with 2 Tbsp. butter until smooth. Set aside and let cool.

2 Add salmon, dill, parsley and scallions to potato mixture and mix well. Taste and season with salt and pepper, if desired. Beat 1 egg; stir into potato mixture. Cover and chill for at least 30 minutes.

3 Divide mixture into 6 even portions and shape into disks. Beat remaining egg. Place flour and bread crumbs in separate shallow bowls. Carefully coat a disk with flour, dusting off excess; dip into beaten egg and then into bread crumbs, patting gently to adhere. Repeat with remaining disks. (Cakes can be kept in refrigerator, covered, until ready to cook, up to 2 days.)

4 Warm oil in a large skillet over medium-low heat. Fry cakes until heated through, 7 to 8 minutes per side, working in batches if necessary.

PER SERVING: 452 Cal., 13g Fat (4g Sat.), 105mg Chol., 4g Fiber, 24g Pro., 63g Carb., 547mg Sod.

Kitchen tips

✳ **Clean up.** If you cook the cakes in batches, wipe the skillet and add more oil in between each batch. This will prevent extra bread crumbs from burning in the bottom of the pan.

✳ **Top it off.** Add a dollop of tartar sauce before serving.

Tuna and Couscous Salad

Prep: 10 min.
Cook: 20 min.
Stand: 15 min.
Serves: 6
Cost per serving:

$1.78

- ¼ cup olive oil
- 3 Tbsp. lemon juice
- 1 clove garlic, finely chopped
- Salt
- 2¼ cups low-sodium chicken broth
- 2 cups Israeli couscous

- 3 cups frozen broccoli florets, thawed
- 2 5-oz. cans tuna packed in water, drained
- ½ cup kalamata olives, pitted and chopped
- ¼ cup finely chopped fresh parsley

1 Whisk together olive oil, lemon juice, garlic and ½ tsp. salt in a small bowl.

2 Bring chicken broth to a boil in a heavy saucepan. Stir in Israeli couscous, cover, reduce heat to low and simmer until tender, 12 to 15 minutes. Transfer couscous to a large cookie sheet; spread out couscous and let cool for 15 minutes.

3 Transfer couscous to a large bowl and stir in broccoli, tuna, olives and parsley. Toss mixture with dressing to coat. Season with additional salt, if desired. Serve salad immediately, or cover and refrigerate for up to 1 day.

PER SERVING: 535 Cal., 13g Fat (1g Sat.), 21mg Chol., 2g Fiber, 32g Pro., 66g Carb., 659mg Sod.

Kitchen tip

✳ **Boost the flavor.** For an even tastier salad, use tuna canned in oil instead of water. Drain the tuna and use the oil in the dressing in place of some of the plain olive oil. Toss in a few chopped sun-dried tomatoes, too.

Shrimp Chowder

Prep: 15 min.
Cook: 30 min.
Serves: 4
Cost per serving:

99¢

- 1 Tbsp. vegetable oil
- 1 medium onion, chopped (about 1 cup)
- 2 ribs celery, chopped (about 1 cup)
- 3 Tbsp. all-purpose flour
- 3 baking potatoes (about 6 oz. each), chopped into ½-inch dice
- 1 8-oz. bottle clam juice
- 1 cup low-sodium chicken broth

- ½ cup half-and-half
- 1 4-oz. can tiny shrimp, not drained
- Salt and pepper

1 In a large pot, warm vegetable oil over medium heat. Add onion and celery and cook, stirring, until vegetables are soft, about 5 minutes. Sprinkle flour over vegetables and sauté 1 minute.

2 Stir in potatoes, clam juice, broth and 2 cups water. Bring just to a boil, reduce heat to medium-low and cook until potatoes are tender, about 12 minutes.

3 Stir in half-and-half and shrimp and cook until heated through, about 5 minutes. Season with salt and pepper and serve hot.

PER SERVING: 240 Cal., 8g Fat (3g Sat.), 84mg Chol., 3g Fiber, 11g Pro., 34g Carb., 923mg Sod.

Tuna and Couscous Salad

Vegetable Couscous with Shrimp

Prep: 20 min.
Cook: 15 min.
Serves: 8
Cost per serving:

97¢

- 2 Tbsp. olive oil
- 1 medium onion, chopped
- 1 small eggplant, cut into ½-inch dice
- 1 zucchini, cut into ½-inch dice
- 1 yellow squash, cut into ½-inch dice
- 2 cloves garlic, minced
- 1 tsp. Italian seasoning
- ½ tsp. salt
- ½ tsp. pepper
- 2 tomatoes, seeded, cut into ½-inch dice
- 1 4-oz. can tiny shrimp, drained and rinsed
- 1 10-oz. box couscous
- 2 Tbsp. chopped fresh parsley, optional

1 Warm oil in a large skillet over medium-high heat. Add onion, eggplant, zucchini and squash. Cook, stirring, until vegetables have softened, about 8 minutes. Add garlic, Italian seasoning, salt and pepper, then sauté 1 minute. Add tomatoes; cook 5 minutes longer, stirring. Stir in shrimp.

2 Bring 2 cups lightly salted water to boil in a pot over high heat. Stir in couscous. Cover pot, remove from heat and let stand until water has absorbed, about 5 minutes. Uncover; fluff couscous with a fork.

3 Divide couscous among 8 plates and spoon shrimp mixture on top. Sprinkle with parsley, if desired, and serve.
PER SERVING: 211 Cal., 4g Fat (1g Sat.), 36mg Chol., 5g Fiber, 9g Pro., 36g Carb., 255mg Sod.

Grilled Tilapia Soft Tacos

from marinade and grill or broil until flaky, 2 to 3 minutes per side. Remove to a plate and let rest for 5 minutes, then cut into chunks. Season with salt, pepper and additional lime juice, if desired.

3 Warm tortillas as package label directs. Serve tilapia in tortillas. Garnish with shredded cheese, avocado chunks, radish slices and cilantro, if desired.

PER SERVING (1 TACO): 144 Cal., 6g Fat (1g Sat.), 36mg Chol., 1g Fiber, 15g Pro., 9g Carb., 159mg Sod.

Kitchen tips

✳ **Give it a kick.** For some extra heat, add a seeded, diced jalapeño to the marinade.

✳ **Watch carefully.** Don't leave the fish in the marinade for more than 30 minutes, or the texture might be mushy. If you would like to work ahead of time, prepare and cook the fish a day in advance, then cover and refrigerate.

✳ **Choose another type of fish.** You can prepare this dish with a different mild fish. Try it with flounder, orange roughy or sole.

Prep: 5 min.
Marinate: 20 min.
Cook: 6 min.
Yield: 16 tacos
Cost per serving:

$1.36

- ¼ cup olive oil
- 2 Tbsp. lime juice
- 2 tsp. soy sauce
- 1 tsp. chili powder
- ½ tsp. cumin
- 1 clove garlic, minced
- 2 lb. tilapia fillets (about 6)
- Salt and pepper
- 16 soft corn tortillas

1 In a small bowl, combine olive oil, lime juice, soy sauce, chili powder, cumin and garlic. Season fish all over with salt and pepper and place in a dish large enough to hold in a single layer. Pour marinade over fish, cover and refrigerate for 15 to 20 minutes.

2 Preheat gas grill to medium, or preheat broiler to high and set rack 6 inches from heat source. Remove fish

Creamy Tuna-and-Mushroom Linguine

Prep: 15 min.

Cook: 25 min.

Serves: 4

Cost per serving:

91¢

- Salt and pepper
- 12 oz. linguine
- 2 Tbsp. unsalted butter
- 2 Tbsp. all-purpose flour
- 1¼ cups milk, warmed
- 1 Tbsp. vegetable oil
- 3 cloves garlic, minced
- 5 oz. mushrooms, sliced (about 1½ cups)
- 1 medium onion, chopped (about 1 cup)
- 2 ribs celery, thinly sliced
- Pinch of crushed red pepper
- 1 5-oz. can water-packed tuna, drained
- Fresh parsley, optional

1 Bring a large pot of salted water to a boil. Cook linguine until al dente, about 9 minutes, or as package label directs. Set aside ½ cup of pasta cooking water, then drain pasta.

2 Melt butter in a small saucepan over medium-low heat. Sprinkle in flour; cook, stirring, until thickened but not browned, 2 minutes. Gradually whisk in warmed milk; continue to whisk until sauce is thick enough to coat the back of a spoon, about 3 minutes. Season with salt and pepper and remove from heat.

3 Warm oil in a large skillet over medium-high heat. Add garlic and cook, stirring, until golden, about 1 minute. Add mushrooms and sauté until they release their liquid and begin to turn golden, about 5 minutes. Add onion, celery and crushed red pepper and cook, stirring, until vegetables are tender, about 5 minutes longer.

4 Stir sauce and reserved pasta water into vegetable mixture and cook, stirring, until heated through, about 5 minutes. Reduce heat to medium-low, add tuna, breaking it up, and cook for 2 minutes. Season with salt and pepper. Toss linguine with sauce, sprinkle with parsley, if desired, and serve hot.

PER SERVING: 521 Cal., 14g Fat (5g Sat.), 42mg Chol., 3g Fiber, 23g Pro., 77g Carb., 559mg Sod.

Baked Fish and Chips

Prep: 10 min.
Bake: 35 min.
Serves: 4
Cost per serving:

$2.76

- 1½ lb. Yukon gold potatoes (about 4), cut in half lengthwise, then each half cut into 4 wedges
- Salt
- 1½ lb. firm fillets of whitefish such as tilapia (thawed if frozen)
- ½ cup all-purpose flour
- 2 large eggs, beaten
- 1½ cups crushed cornflakes (from about 3 cups cornflakes)

1 Arrange 2 racks in top and bottom thirds of oven and preheat to 450°F. Line 2 rimmed baking sheets with heavy-duty foil. Mist one sheet with cooking spray. Top second sheet with a wire rack and mist rack with cooking spray.

2 Arrange potatoes on first baking sheet and coat with a layer of cooking spray. Sprinkle potatoes with salt.

Bake potatoes in bottom third of oven until undersides are golden, 15 to 20 minutes.

3 While potatoes are baking, sprinkle both sides of fish with salt, dredge in flour and dip into eggs, letting excess drip off. Coat fish with crushed cornflakes. Place fish on wire rack set on second baking sheet. Mist fish with cooking spray.

4 Turn potatoes, return to bottom third of oven. Place fish in top third of oven. Bake until potatoes are golden and fish is cooked through, about 15 minutes longer. Serve immediately.

PER SERVING: 464 Cal., 6g Fat (2g Sat.), 191mg Chol., 5g Fiber, 44g Pro., 60g Carb., 624mg Sod.

Kitchen tip

✳ **Switch fish.** Use another variety of whitefish, such as flounder or halibut, if you prefer. Thicker fillets probably will take a couple of minutes longer to cook through than thinner ones.

*Salmon, Potato
and Green Bean Salad*

Salmon, Potato and Green Bean Salad

Prep: 10 min.
Cook: 12 min.
Serves: 4
Cost per serving:

$3.31

- **2 medium red potatoes (about 12 oz.), thinly sliced**
- **Salt and pepper**

- **1 lb. salmon fillet, skin removed**
- **8 oz. green beans, trimmed**
- **⅓ cup pitted black olives, chopped**
- **2 Tbsp. olive oil**
- **2 Tbsp. lemon juice**

1 Bring 1 inch of water to a boil in a pan. Line with parchment a steamer basket that will fit in pan. Arrange potatoes in basket; sprinkle with salt. Place salmon over potatoes; sprinkle with salt. Lower steamer into pan (don't let basket touch water). Steam for 6 minutes. Place green beans over salmon, cover and continue steaming until potatoes and beans are tender and fish is cooked through, 4 to 6 minutes longer.

2 Transfer potatoes, beans and salmon to a large bowl. Flake salmon. Allow food to cool slightly, then add olives to bowl, drizzle with oil and lemon juice, season with salt and pepper and serve.
PER SERVING: 317 Cal., 16g Fat (2g Sat.), 62mg Chol., 3g Fiber, 25g Pro., 18g Carb., 425mg Sod.

Tuna and Macaroni Salad

Prep: 15 min.
Cook: 10 min.
Serves: 8
Cost per serving:

80¢

- **Salt and pepper**
- **1 lb. elbow macaroni**
- **3 ribs celery, finely chopped**
- **½ red onion, finely diced**
- **½ cup finely chopped fresh parsley**
- **1 carrot, grated**
- **1 12-oz. can tuna in water, drained**
- **½ cup plus 2 Tbsp. reduced-fat mayonnaise**
- **¼ cup plain low-fat yogurt**
- **1 Tbsp. plus 1 tsp. cider vinegar**

1 Bring a large pot of salted water to a boil. Add macaroni and cook until al dente, about 10 minutes, or as package label directs. Drain, rinse with cold water and drain again thoroughly.

2 While pasta is cooking, combine celery, onion, parsley, carrot and tuna in a large bowl. Add cooled macaroni and toss to combine. In a small bowl, whisk together mayonnaise, yogurt and vinegar. Season with salt and pepper and whisk to combine. Pour mayonnaise mixture over pasta and toss until well coated. Cover and refrigerate until ready to serve.
PER SERVING: 312 Cal., 4g Fat (0g Sat.), 19mg Chol., 3g Fiber, 18g Pro., 48g Carb., 520mg Sod.

Kitchen tips

✳ **Add more veggies.** Toss in roasted red peppers, chopped artichoke hearts or sun-dried tomatoes.

✳ **Trade pastas.** Elbow macaroni is traditional, but you can use any short pasta shape in this recipe.

Soy-Glazed Shrimp Kebabs

Soy-Glazed Shrimp Kebabs

Prep: 30 min.
Cook: 22 min.
Yield: 8 kebabs
Cost per serving:

$3.44

- ½ cup apple juice
- ¼ cup soy sauce
- 1 Tbsp. cider vinegar
- 2 Tbsp. sugar
- 12 slices bacon (about 8 oz.)
- 1½ lb. medium shrimp, peeled and deveined
- 8 oz. snow peas, strings removed
- 1 red bell pepper, stemmed, seeded and cut into 1-inch pieces

1 Combine apple juice, soy sauce, vinegar and sugar in a small saucepan. Bring to a boil over high heat. Reduce heat to medium-low and simmer until thickened and syrupy, about 15 minutes. Remove from heat and cool to room temperature.

2 While glaze is cooking, preheat oven to 400°F. Line a rimmed baking sheet with foil and place a cooling rack on top. Lay bacon in a single layer on top of cooling rack; roast for 15 minutes. Remove to a paper towel–lined plate to cool.

3 Stack 4 slices of bacon and cut into 8 1-inch squares. Repeat with remaining bacon. (You should end up with 24 stacks of 4 layers, or 3 stacks per skewer.)

4 Preheat broiler or set a gas grill to medium. Thread shrimp onto 8 long metal skewers, alternating with snow peas, peppers and stacks of bacon.

5 Set broiling pan about 6 inches from heat source or oil grill grates. Brush each skewer with soy glaze and broil or grill, turning often, until shrimp is pink throughout and bacon is browned and sizzling, about 7 minutes. Serve kebabs warm.

PER SERVING (1 KEBAB): 272 Cal., 19g Fat (5g Sat.), 160mg Chol., 1g Fiber, 27g Pro., 10g Carb., 913mg Sod.

Salmon-Spinach Frittata

Prep: 10 min.
Cook: 20 min.
Serves: 8
Cost per serving:

$1.08

- 3 Tbsp. olive oil
- 1 onion, chopped
- 1 red bell pepper, seeded, thinly sliced
- 1 10-oz. package frozen spinach, thawed, squeezed dry
- 1 7.5-oz. can salmon, drained
- Salt and pepper
- 8 large eggs, lightly beaten

1 Warm oil over medium heat in a 12-inch nonstick skillet with an ovenproof handle. Add onion and bell pepper and sauté for 5 minutes. Add spinach and salmon; season with salt and pepper and sauté until heated through.

2 Preheat broiler to high; set an oven rack 5 inches from heat source. Pour eggs into skillet; stir to distribute vegetables and salmon. Reduce heat to medium-low and cook, sliding a spatula under frittata occasionally to loosen, until set underneath but still wet on top, about 8 minutes.

3 Place skillet under broiler; cook until top is golden brown, 1 to 2 minutes. Slide frittata onto a platter, cut and serve.

PER SERVING: 168 Cal., 11g Fat (3g Sat.), 221mg Chol., 2g Fiber, 13g Pro., 5g Carb., 382mg Sod.

Tortellini and White Bean Soup

Vegetables

Slow-Cooker Eggplant and Tomato Sauce with Pasta

on low until eggplant is soft and sauce is thick, 5 to 7 hours.

2 Bring a large pot of salted water to a boil over high heat. Add pasta and cook until al dente, about 10 minutes. Drain pasta, toss with sauce and serve.

PER SERVING: 376 Cal., 2g Fat (0g Sat.), 0mg Chol., 7g Fiber, 13g Pro., 77g Carb., 697mg Sod.

Kitchen tips

✳ **Dress it up.** You can give the sauce even more flavor by stirring in ¼ cup chopped fresh basil or sprinkling with grated Parmesan.

✳ **Store it.** This sauce freezes well, so make extra (without the pasta), then divide it into single-serving containers and freeze. Be sure to label the containers with the contents and date.

✳ **Make it a meal.** A green salad rounds out this vegetarian supper. To make it heartier, add 1 or 2 cans of white beans (rinsed and drained) to the slow cooker for the last 30 minutes of cooking.

Prep: 10 min.
Cook: 7 hr.
Serves: 6
Cost per serving:

$1.30

- 1 28-oz. can diced tomatoes, drained
- 1 6-oz. can tomato paste
- ½ cup red wine or water
- 1 medium eggplant (about 1 lb.), cut into ½-inch cubes
- 1 onion, finely chopped
- 1 tsp. dried oregano
- 2 cloves garlic, finely chopped
- Salt
- 1 lb. penne or other short pasta

1 Combine tomatoes, tomato paste, wine or water, eggplant, onion, oregano, garlic and ½ tsp. salt in slow cooker. Cover and cook

ANTONIS ACHILLEOS; FOOD STYLING: SUSAN VAJARANANT

Kitchen tip

❋ **Change the flavors.** You can make a few swaps to suit your tastes. Try Cheddar or plain Monterey Jack instead of the pepper Jack. Use fat-free canned refried beans or mash some kidney beans in place of the black beans. Add a few shakes of hot sauce.

Cheesy Corn-and-Black-Bean Quesadillas

Prep: 15 min.
Cook: 25 min.
Serves: 8
Cost per serving:

80¢

- 1 15.5-oz. can black beans, rinsed and drained
- 1½ cups frozen corn kernels, thawed
- 1 Tbsp. canola oil
- 1 small onion, chopped
- 1 jalapeño, seeded and finely chopped
- 2 cloves garlic, minced
- 6 oz. pepper Jack, shredded
- Salt and pepper
- 8 8-inch flour tortillas

1 In a bowl, coarsely mash black beans with a potato masher. Warm a large skillet over medium-high heat; add corn and cook, stirring occasionally, until corn begins to brown, 3 to 4 minutes. Add corn to bowl with beans.

2 In same skillet, warm oil. Add onion and jalapeño and sauté for 2 minutes. Add garlic and sauté 1 minute longer. Stir mixture into bowl with beans and corn. Let mixture cool to room temperature, about 10 minutes.

3 When bean mixture is cool, stir in cheese and season with salt and pepper. Preheat oven to 200°F. Place a tortilla on a work surface and spread ½ cup bean mixture over lower half. Fold tortilla in half. Repeat with remaining tortillas and bean mixture.

4 Warm a large skillet over medium-high heat. Cook as many quesadillas as can fit in skillet for 3 minutes, then flip quesadillas and cook until golden brown and crispy and cheese is melting, 2 to 3 minutes longer. Place quesadillas on a baking sheet and keep warm in oven as you cook remaining quesadillas. Cut into wedges and serve.
PER SERVING: 305 Cal., 12g Fat (6g Sat.), 19mg Chol., 5g Fiber, 12g Pro., 40g Carb., 789mg Sod.

Whole-Wheat Pasta with White Beans and Spinach

Prep: 5 min.
Cook: 12 min.
Serves: 6
Cost per serving:

82¢

- Salt
- 1 lb. whole-wheat penne
- 2 Tbsp. olive oil
- ¼ cup seasoned bread crumbs
- 2 cloves garlic, chopped

- 1 15-oz. can white beans, drained and rinsed
- 10 oz. baby spinach (about 5 cups)
- ½ cup low-sodium chicken broth

1 Bring a large pot of salted water to a boil. Add pasta and cook until al dente, about 10 minutes or as package label directs.

2 Warm 1 Tbsp. oil in a small skillet over medium heat.

Add bread crumbs and ¼ tsp. salt and cook, stirring occasionally, until toasted, about 5 minutes. Transfer to a small bowl.

3 Warm remaining 1 Tbsp. olive oil in a large skillet over medium-high heat. Add garlic and sauté until fragrant, about 30 seconds. Stir in beans, spinach and broth; bring to a boil. Lower heat and simmer until spinach has wilted, 2 to 3 minutes.

4 Drain pasta, reserving ½ cup cooking water. Toss pasta with bean mixture, stirring in reserved water about 1 Tbsp. at a time, if needed, to reach desired consistency. Season with salt. Divide pasta equally among 6 bowls and sprinkle each portion with bread crumbs.

PER SERVING: 441 Cal., 7g Fat (1g Sat.), 0mg Chol., 12g Fiber, 17g Pro., 78g Carb., 341mg Sod.

Black Bean and Mango Tostadas

Prep: 5 min.
Cook: 10 min.
Serves: 4
Cost per serving:

$1.54

- 1 15-oz. can black beans, drained and rinsed
- 1 Tbsp. olive oil
- 2 scallions, white and light green parts, finely chopped
- ½ tsp. chili powder
- ¾ tsp. salt
- 4 8-inch flour tortillas
- 6 oz. grated low-fat Monterey Jack
- 1 ripe mango, peeled, pitted and diced
- ¼ small red onion, finely chopped (about 2 Tbsp.)
- 1 Tbsp. lime juice

1 Preheat oven to 425°F. Combine beans, olive oil, scallions, chili powder and ½ tsp. salt in a bowl.

2 Mist a baking sheet with cooking spray. Place tortillas on sheet and spoon bean mixture on top. Sprinkle with cheese. Bake tostadas until golden and crisp, about 10 minutes.

3 While tostadas are baking, combine mango, onion, lime juice and ¼ tsp. salt in a bowl. Remove tostadas from oven, spoon mango mixture on top and serve.

PER SERVING: 392 Cal., 16g Fat (7g Sat.), 30mg Chol., 8g Fiber, 19g Pro., 50g Carb., 1,496mg Sod.

Kitchen tips

❋ **Spice it up.** If you like more heat, use pepper Jack cheese instead of plain Monterey Jack.

❋ **Swap salsas.** Don't care for mango or can't find one? Sub in tomato salsa instead, or try a jarred tomatillo salsa.

❋ **Go green.** To add another layer of flavor, sprinkle on some chopped avocado and fresh cilantro before serving.

❋ **Put in more fruit.** Mango gives the dish a touch of sweetness. You can substitute or add

chopped papaya, pineapple or kiwi for an even greater tropical taste.

❋ **Try another base.** Small flour tortillas were used to assemble these tostadas, but you may go with corn tortillas if you prefer.

Curried Pumpkin Soup with Spicy Pumpkin Seeds

Prep: 15 min.
Cook: 35 min.
Serves: 6
Cost per serving:

$1.67

PUMPKIN SEEDS:
- ¼ tsp. cayenne
- ½ tsp. sugar
- ¼ tsp. salt
- 2 tsp. unsalted butter
- ½ cup raw pumpkin seeds

SOUP:
- 2 Tbsp. unsalted butter
- 1 small onion, finely chopped (about 1 cup)
- 2 medium Golden Delicious apples, peeled, cored, finely chopped
- 2 Tbsp. minced fresh ginger
- 2 Tbsp. all-purpose flour
- 1 tsp. cumin
- 2 Tbsp. curry powder
- ⅛ tsp. chili powder
- 3 cups low-sodium chicken broth
- 2 15-oz. cans pumpkin
- 1 13.6-oz. can light unsweetened coconut milk
- Salt and pepper
- Plain yogurt, for serving, optional

1 Prepare seeds: Mix cayenne, sugar and salt. Melt butter in a skillet over medium heat. Add seeds; sauté 3 minutes. Add spices; sauté until seeds are toasted, 2 to 3 minutes. Remove to a bowl.

2 Make soup: Melt butter in a large pot over medium heat. Add onion, apples and ginger and sauté until tender, about 8 minutes. Sprinkle flour, cumin and curry and chili powders on top; stir for 1 minute.

3 Whisk in broth and cook, stirring, until soup begins to thicken, about 6 minutes. Whisk in pumpkin and coconut milk. Season with salt and pepper. Bring to a low boil and cook for 5 minutes, stirring. Reduce heat; simmer for 10 minutes. Remove from heat and let cool.

4 Working in batches, puree soup in a blender until smooth. Return to pot to reheat. Serve hot, topped with yogurt, if desired, and pumpkin seeds.

PER SERVING: 261 Cal., 17g Fat (8g Sat.), 14mg Chol., 8g Fiber, 8g Pro., 25g Carb., 584mg Sod.

Broccoli-and-Cheese-Stuffed Baked Potatoes

Prep: 15 min.
Bake: 2 hr.
Serves: 8
Cost per serving:

$1.85

- 8 large baking potatoes
- 2 Tbsp. olive oil
- ¾ lb. broccoli florets
- 1 large onion, finely chopped
- 4 cloves garlic, minced
- 2 cups grated low-fat Cheddar
- ½ cup sour cream
- ¼ cup milk
- Salt and pepper

1 Preheat oven to 375°F. Rub potatoes with 1 Tbsp. oil; pierce with a knife. Bake until tender, about 1 hour and 30 minutes. Steam broccoli until tender, about 5 minutes. Drain and rinse broccoli. Pat dry and roughly chop.

2 In a skillet over low heat, warm 1 Tbsp. oil. Sauté onion until soft, about 10 minutes. Add garlic; sauté for 2 minutes longer.

3 Set oven to 350°F. Cut top ¼ inch off potato. Scoop out flesh; mash flesh. Mix with vegetables, Cheddar, sour cream and milk. Season with salt and pepper. Stuff shells and bake for 30 minutes.

PER SERVING: 231 Cal., 9g Fat (4g Sat.), 17mg Chol., 9g Fiber, 16g Pro., 25g Carb., 364mg Sod.

*Curried Pumpkin Soup
with Spicy Pumpkin Seeds*

❋ **Swap vegetables.**
You can use any combination of veggies in this flexible recipe. Spinach works nicely, but be sure to sauté until wilted (or defrost completely if frozen) and squeeze out as much excess water as possible.

❋ **Turn up the heat.**
If your family likes a spicy kick, finely dice a jalapeño and sauté with the scallions. Remove the seeds, though, or it will be too hot.

Vegetable-Cheddar Strata

Prep: 40 min.

Chill: 4 hr.

Stand: 30 min.

Bake: 1 hr.

Serves: 8

Cost per serving:

$1.67

- 1 Tbsp. olive oil
- 6 scallions, white and light-green parts only, chopped
- Salt and pepper
- 2 cups broccoli florets, chopped
- 1 small red bell pepper, seeded and finely chopped
- 2 cloves garlic, minced
- 5 whole-wheat English muffins, split, toasted and quartered
- 2½ cups shredded reduced-fat sharp Cheddar
- 8 large eggs
- 2½ cups whole milk
- 2 Tbsp. Dijon mustard
- ½ tsp. hot sauce, optional

1 In a large skillet over medium-high heat, warm oil. Add scallions, sprinkle with salt and sauté until tender, about 2 minutes. Add broccoli, bell pepper and garlic; cook, stirring often, until vegetables are tender, about 5 minutes. Transfer to a bowl and season with salt and pepper.

2 Mist a 9-by-13-inch baking dish with cooking spray. Arrange English muffin pieces on bottom of dish, cut sides up. Scatter vegetable mixture over muffins; sprinkle with 2 cups cheese.

3 In a large bowl, whisk eggs, milk, mustard and hot sauce, if desired; season generously with salt and pepper. Pour egg mixture evenly over vegetable mixture in baking dish. Cover with plastic wrap and refrigerate for at least 4 hours or overnight.

4 Let strata stand at room temperature for 30 minutes before baking. Preheat oven to 375°F; line a large rimmed baking sheet with foil. Remove plastic wrap from baking dish and cover with foil. Place dish on baking sheet; bake for 30 minutes. Remove foil, sprinkle with remaining ½ cup cheese and bake until golden and just set in center, 20 to 30 minutes longer. Let stand on a wire rack for 10 minutes before serving.

PER SERVING: 340 Cal., 18g Fat (8g Sat.), 247mg Chol., 4g Fiber, 22g Pro., 26g Carb., 906mg Sod.

Spaghetti with Butternut Squash

a single layer and roast until soft, stirring occasionally, about 25 minutes.

2 Bring a large pot of salted water to a boil. Cook spaghetti until just tender, about 10 minutes, or as package label directs. Drain, reserving ½ cup of pasta cooking water. Return spaghetti to pot and add butter, sage and squash. Stir, adding pasta water as necessary to moisten. Top with Parmesan and serve.

PER SERVING: 428 Cal., 11g Fat (4g Sat.), 14mg Chol., 4g Fiber, 12g Pro., 71g Carb., 263mg Sod.

Kitchen tips

✳ **Switch noodles.** This dish works equally well with penne or linguine.

✳ **Save time.** Look for pre-peeled chunks of butternut squash in your grocery store's produce section. You will need about 2½ cups of cubed squash for this recipe.

Prep: 15 min.
Cook: 30 min.
Serves: 6
Cost per serving:

69¢

- 1 small butternut squash (about 1½ lb.), peeled, seeded, cut into ½-inch cubes
- 2 Tbsp. olive oil
- Salt
- 1 lb. spaghetti
- 2 Tbsp. unsalted butter, melted
- 2 Tbsp. finely chopped fresh sage
- ¼ cup grated Parmesan

1 Preheat oven to 400°F. Line a baking sheet with heavy-duty aluminum foil. On baking sheet, toss squash with oil and ¼ tsp. salt to coat. Spread squash in

Tortellini and White Bean Soup

Prep: 10 min.
Cook: 15 min.
Serves: 4
Cost per serving:

$2.30

- 1 Tbsp. olive oil
- 2 ribs celery, sliced
- 1 15-oz. can diced tomatoes, drained
- ½ tsp. dried oregano
- 2 cloves garlic, minced
- 6 cups low-sodium chicken broth
- 1 8-oz. package fresh cheese or meat tortellini
- 1 15-oz. can white beans, drained and rinsed
- Salt, optional
- ¼ cup grated Parmesan

1 Warm olive oil in a large saucepan over medium-high heat. Add celery, tomatoes and oregano and cook, stirring occasionally, until celery begins to soften, about 3 minutes. Add garlic and cook, stirring constantly, until fragrant, about 2 minutes longer.

2 Stir in broth and bring soup to a boil. Carefully add tortellini and beans and cook, stirring occasionally, until soup is heated through and tortellini are tender, about 7 minutes. Season with salt, if desired.

3 Using a ladle, divide soup among 4 bowls. Sprinkle each bowl of soup with 1 Tbsp. Parmesan and serve immediately.

PER SERVING: 383 Cal., 10g Fat (4g Sat.), 20mg Chol., 7g Fiber, 24g Pro., 53g Carb., 760mg Sod.

Kitchen tip

✳ **Select another pasta.** Use spinach tortellini for an extra boost of green.

Spinach and Feta Quesadillas

Prep: 10 min.

Cook: 32 min.

Serves: 4

Cost per serving:

$1.82

- **1 Tbsp. olive oil**
- **½ small onion, finely chopped**
- **1 10-oz. package frozen spinach, thawed and squeezed dry**
- **6 oz. feta, crumbled**
- **¼ cup kalamata or other black olives, pitted and chopped**
- **4 10-inch flour tortillas**

1 Warm oil in a medium skillet over medium-high heat. Add onion and cook, stirring, until softened, about 3 minutes. Stir in spinach and cook, stirring, until heated through, 2 to 3 minutes longer. Transfer to a bowl and stir in cheese and olives.

2 Spread a quarter of spinach mixture over half of each tortilla. Fold to cover; press lightly to seal.

3 Place a large skillet over medium-high heat. Cook quesadillas one at a time in skillet, turning once, until golden on both sides and cheese is melted, about 6 minutes total for each. Serve immediately.

PER SERVING: 339 Cal., 20g Fat (8g Sat.), 38mg Chol., 5g Fiber, 15g Pro., 43g Carb., 1,046mg Sod.

Kitchen tips

❊ **Shake it off.** Don't add any salt to the vegetables when sautéing them. The olives and feta are both salty enough on their own. Offer salsa on the side.

❊ **Change cheeses.** Try these easy quesadillas with Monterey Jack or Cheddar.

❊ **Build it up.** Sautéed mushrooms add more vitamins and a hearty meatiness to this dish. Slice button or cremini mushrooms and sauté them before the onions. Be sure to keep sautéing until mushrooms release their liquid, which takes about 7 minutes.

❊ **Make it healthier.** Use whole-grain tortillas to add nutrients to these family-pleasing quesadillas.

Pizza with Fresh Tomatoes and Basil

Pizza with Fresh Tomatoes and Basil

Prep: 15 min.
Bake: 25 min.
Serves: 4
Cost per serving:

$1.76

- **1 lb. frozen pizza dough, thawed in refrigerator**
- **½ cup jarred marinara sauce**
- **¾ cup shredded part-skim mozzarella**
- **1 medium tomato, seeded and chopped**
- **8 fresh basil leaves**

1 Preheat oven to 400°F. Shape dough into a disk. On a lightly floured countertop, roll out or stretch dough to a 12-inch circle. Fold in edges to form a ½-inch rim. Transfer dough to a pizza pan or large baking sheet lined with parchment. Prick dough several times with a fork.

2 Spread marinara sauce evenly over dough, sprinkle mozzarella on top of sauce and place tomato slices all over. Bake until pizza crust is golden brown, 20 to 25 minutes. Just before serving, sprinkle basil leaves over pizza. Cut pizza into wedges and serve hot.

PER SERVING: 391 Cal., 9g Fat (4g Sat.), 11mg Chol., 3g Fiber, 13g Pro., 59g Carb., 795mg Sod.

Kitchen tips

✳ **Keep it green.** Don't add the basil to the pizza until you're ready to serve it. If the leaves sit on the hot pizza for more than a couple of minutes, they will turn black.

✳ **Add toppings.** Pile on crumbled cooked turkey sausage, olives, roasted red peppers or mushrooms.

Black Bean and Butternut Squash Chili

Prep: 20 min.
Cook: 6 hr.
Serves: 8
Cost per serving:

$1.94

- **¼ cup olive oil**
- **3 onions, chopped**
- **4 cloves garlic, minced**
- **1 red bell pepper, seeded and chopped**
- **1 green bell pepper, seeded and chopped**
- **2 jalapeños, seeded and minced**
- **4 15-oz. cans black beans, rinsed and drained**
- **2 14.5-oz. cans diced fire-roasted tomatoes**
- **3 Tbsp. chili powder**
- **2 Tbsp. cumin**
- **1 Tbsp. dried oregano**
- **4 cups butternut squash (about 2 lb.), peeled, seeded and cut into ½-inch dice**
- **Salt and pepper**

1 Warm olive oil in a large skillet over medium heat. Sauté onions until tender, about 3 minutes. Add garlic and sauté for 1 minute. Add bell peppers and jalapeños and sauté until tender, about 3 minutes longer.

2 Transfer pepper mixture to slow cooker. Stir in black beans, tomatoes, chili powder, cumin and oregano. Arrange butternut squash on top. Cover and cook on low for 6 hours.

3 Season chili with salt and pepper. Serve with sour cream, salsa, chopped scallions and other toppings, if desired.

PER SERVING: 276 Cal., 8g Fat (1g Sat.), 0mg Chol., 16g Fiber, 11g Pro., 50g Carb., 1,190mg Sod.

Broiled Eggplant Parmesan

eggplant until golden brown, turning once, 10 to 12 minutes total.

3 Remove baking sheet from oven. Spoon tomato puree over each slice, sprinkle with both cheeses and top with bread crumbs. Return to oven and broil until cheese is melted and bread crumbs are toasted, 1 to 2 minutes. Serve immediately.

PER SERVING: 266 Cal., 11g Fat (7g Sat.), 29mg Chol., 9g Fiber, 18g Pro., 26g Carb., 1,125mg Sod.

Kitchen tips

* **Be fresh.** For an extra shot of color and flavor, sprinkle chopped fresh basil over the eggplant just before serving.

* **Choose sides.** Enjoy this easy vegetarian dish with pasta and a salad for a complete meal. Or make it a side dish with grilled Italian turkey sausages.

* **Get creative.** If you don't have any Italian-seasoned bread crumbs, mix plain ones with a few dried herbs such as oregano, parsley and thyme.

Prep: 10 min.
Cook: 15 min.
Serves: 4
Cost per serving:

$1.58

- 1 15-oz. can diced tomatoes
- 2 medium eggplants (about 2 lb.), ends

trimmed, cut into ⅓-inch-thick slices
- **Salt and pepper**
- **6 oz. part-skim mozzarella, shredded**
- **¼ cup grated Parmesan**
- **⅓ cup Italian-seasoned bread crumbs**

1 Preheat broiler to high; place a rack about 8 inches from heat source. Line a rimmed

baking sheet with heavy-duty aluminum foil and mist with cooking spray. Drain tomatoes, discarding liquid. Puree tomatoes in a blender or food processor. Set aside.

2 Mist eggplant slices on both sides with cooking spray, sprinkle with salt and pepper and set in a single layer on lined baking sheet. Broil

Kitchen tips

✳ Change the flavor. Tomato salsa works well with black beans, but you can also try a different type. Chipotle salsa lends a smoky taste to this dish. Or you can try a pineapple or mango salsa for a touch of sweetness.

✳ Use more veggies. Sauté a chopped onion and a diced, seeded jalapeño until tender and stir them into the beans before sprinkling the cheese on top.

✳ Make it meaty. This is a warming vegetarian meal, but you can please meat eaters by cooking a few slices of bacon until crisp and crumbling them into the slow cooker with the beans before cooking.

Easy Mexican Black Bean Casserole

Prep: 5 min.
Cook: 6 hr. 10 min.
Serves: 6
Cost per serving:

$1.31

- **16 oz. dried black beans, picked over**
- **1 16-oz. jar salsa, plus extra for serving, optional**
- **Salt**
- **6 oz. shredded Cheddar or Monterey Jack**
- **Tortilla chips for serving, optional**

1 Stir together black beans, salsa and 4 cups water in slow cooker. Cover and cook on high until liquid has absorbed and beans are soft, 4 to 6 hours.

2 Season with salt. Sprinkle shredded cheese over beans, cover and continue to cook until cheese has melted, 5 to 10 minutes. Spoon into bowls. Top with additional salsa and serve with tortilla chips, if desired.

PER SERVING: 398 Cal., 9g Fat (5g Sat.), 30mg Chol., 20g Fiber, 24g Pro., 56g Carb., 982mg Sod.

Vegetable Fried Rice

Prep: 5 min.
Cook: 10 min.
Serves: 4
Cost per serving:

$1.08

- 3 Tbsp. soy sauce
- 1 tsp. sugar
- ¼ cup vegetable oil
- 3 large eggs, lightly beaten
- 3 cloves garlic, minced
- 2 tsp. minced, peeled fresh ginger
- 5 cups cold cooked rice
- ½ tsp. salt
- 4 scallions, white and light green parts, chopped
- 1 12-oz. bag mixed frozen vegetables, such as Birds Eye Asian Medley
- 2 tsp. sesame oil

1 In a small bowl, stir together soy sauce and sugar. Warm 2 Tbsp. vegetable oil in a wok or large nonstick skillet over medium-high heat. Add eggs and cook, stirring once or twice, until just set. Transfer to a small bowl and wipe out skillet.

2 Warm remaining 2 Tbsp. vegetable oil in same skillet. Sauté garlic and ginger for 30 seconds. Add rice and salt; stir-fry until heated through and starting to crisp, 3 to 4 minutes. Add soy sauce mixture, scallions and vegetables; stir-fry until heated through, 3 to 5 minutes. Return eggs to skillet and stir-fry until just combined. Drizzle with sesame oil and serve.
PER SERVING: 547 Cal., 18g Fat (2g Sat.), 159mg Chol., 3g Fiber, 13g Pro., 80g Carb., 1,063mg Sod.

Kitchen tips

✳ **Get a head start.**
If you make extra rice early in the week you will be halfway there when you begin to cook this quick dinner.

✳ **Make it healthier.**
For a nutrient boost, go with brown rice instead of white.

✳ **Use leftovers.**
Have chicken, pork or steak left over from another meal? Cut it into chunks and add it to this flavorful dish.

Tomato, Basil and Red Pepper Soup

Prep: 10 min.

Cook: 20 min.

Serves: 6

Cost per serving:

$1.29

- 2 Tbsp. unsalted butter
- 4 scallions, thinly sliced
- 1 28-oz. can diced tomatoes
- 1¾ cups low-sodium chicken broth
- 1 cup chopped jarred roasted red bell peppers, rinsed and seeded
- ¾ tsp. dried basil
- Salt and pepper
- ¾ cup heavy cream

1 Melt butter over medium-low heat in a large saucepan or pot. Add scallions and cook, stirring occasionally, until scallions begin to soften, about 4 minutes. Stir in tomatoes with their liquid, chicken broth, roasted peppers and basil. Season with salt and pepper.

2 Increase heat to high and bring mixture to a boil. Reduce heat and simmer, stirring occasionally, about 10 minutes. Remove from heat, stir in heavy cream and season with salt and pepper. Serve hot.

PER SERVING: 196 Cal., 16g Fat (9g Sat.), 53mg Chol., 1g Fiber, 3g Pro., 10g Carb., 472mg Sod.

Kitchen tips

✳ **Punch it up.** Try a flavored olive oil (in place of butter) or flavored diced tomatoes for a stronger taste.

✳ **Bring on the sides.** Serve the soup with a green salad or with grilled cheese sandwiches. Or hollow out 6 small round whole-wheat or sourdough loaves and ladle the soup into them. Serve on plates.

✳ **Add more protein.** You can give the soup additional heft by sautéing 1 pound of lean ground beef or turkey instead of the butter. When the meat is no longer pink, drain off any excess fat, add the scallions and continue following the recipe.

Slow-Cooker Tuscan Beans

Prep: 5 min.
Cook: 3 hr. 15 min.
Serves: 6
Cost per serving:

39¢

- **1 lb. dried cannellini beans, rinsed and picked over**
- **6 cloves garlic, crushed**
- **1 sprig fresh sage**
- **Salt and pepper**
- **6 tsp. extra-virgin olive oil**

1 Combine beans, garlic, sage, 1 tsp. salt and 8 cups water in slow cooker. Cover and cook on high until beans are tender, about 3 hours and 15 minutes.

2 Drain beans and discard garlic and sage. Season beans generously with salt and pepper. Spoon beans into bowls and drizzle each portion with 1 tsp. olive oil.
PER SERVING: 290 Cal., 5g Fat (1g Sat.), 0mg Chol., 12g Fiber, 18g Pro., 43g Carb., 211mg Sod.

Kitchen tips

❋ **Round it out.** Serve the beans the Tuscan way, with crusty bread and a green salad.

❋ **Try another bean.** You may use Great Northern or navy beans in this recipe.

Vegetable Soup

Prep: 15 min.
Cook: 30 min.
Serves: 6
Cost per serving:

$1.72

- **2 Tbsp. canola oil**
- **2 carrots, cut into ½-inch dice**
- **1 large onion, chopped**
- **1 rib celery, thinly sliced**
- **1 clove garlic, minced**
- **1 14.5-oz. can diced tomatoes, drained**
- **2 small Yukon gold or red potatoes (about 4 oz. each), cut into ½-inch dice**
- **6 cups low-sodium vegetable broth**
- **1 small zucchini, cut into ½-inch dice**
- **1 small yellow squash, cut into ½-inch dice**

- **1 cup broccoli florets, cut into small pieces**
- **Salt and pepper**
- **¾ cup grated Parmesan**
- **Chopped fresh herbs**

such as thyme, parsley or basil, optional

1 Warm oil in a large saucepan over medium-high heat.

Add carrots, onion and celery; cook, stirring often, until vegetables are slightly softened, about 3 minutes. Add garlic; sauté 1 minute longer. Stir in tomatoes and potatoes. Pour in broth and bring to a boil. Reduce heat to low and simmer, uncovered, until flavors have blended and potatoes are slightly softened, about 10 minutes.

2 Add zucchini, squash and broccoli and continue to cook until potatoes are cooked through and vegetables are tender but not mushy, about 7 minutes. Season soup with salt and pepper. Sprinkle with Parmesan and herbs, if desired. Serve hot.
PER SERVING: 183 Cal., 8g Fat (3g Sat.), 11mg Chol., 4g Fiber, 8g Pro., 19g Carb., 628mg Sod.

Slow-Cooker Tuscan Beans

Spinach and Potato Pizza

Spinach and Potato Pizza

Prep: 15 min.
Bake: 20 min.
Serves: 4
Cost per serving:

$2.52

- 2 Tbsp. olive oil
- 1 lb. frozen pizza dough, thawed
- 8 oz. Yukon gold potatoes, thinly sliced
- ½ tsp. salt
- 1 10-oz. package frozen chopped spinach, thawed and squeezed dry
- 8 oz. shredded Gruyère

1 Preheat oven to 475°F. Brush bottom of a 16-by-11-inch rimmed baking sheet with 1 Tbsp. olive oil. Press and stretch dough evenly to cover bottom of baking sheet. (If at first dough resists, let it rest for a few minutes before continuing.) Toss potatoes with 1 Tbsp. olive oil and spread potatoes over dough. Sprinkle with salt. Scatter spinach over potatoes. Sprinkle with Gruyère.

2 Bake until underside of crust is golden (lift an edge of pizza carefully with a spatula to peek) and cheese is bubbling, about 20 minutes. Let stand 5 minutes on a wire rack before slicing.
PER SERVING: 679 Cal., 29g Fat (12g Sat.), 62mg Chol., 5g Fiber, 31g Pro., 75g Carb., 1,089mg Sod.

Kitchen tips

✳ **Change cheeses.** If Gruyère is too strong, substitute Jack cheese. Or, give the pizza Greek flair with crumbled feta. Sprinkle on chopped sun-dried tomatoes and oregano, too.

✳ **Keep the skins.** Yukon gold potatoes have thin skins, so feel free to leave them on for added fiber.

Loaded Nachos

Prep: 10 min.
Cook: 10 min.
Serves: 4
Cost per serving:

$1.56

- 24 large baked tortilla chips (about 3 oz.)
- 2 tsp. canola oil
- 1 onion, chopped
- 1 clove garlic, minced
- ½ tsp. chili powder
- ½ cup canned black beans (rinse and drain before measuring)
- ½ cup cherry tomatoes, halved or quartered
- 2 tsp. lemon juice
- ¼ cup chopped fresh cilantro
- Salt and pepper
- ½ cup shredded low-fat Cheddar
- ½ avocado, diced
- ½ cup reduced-fat Greek yogurt

1 Preheat broiler to high. Line a broiling pan or large, rimmed baking sheet with foil and mist with cooking spray. Arrange chips, overlapping slightly, in a single layer on foil.

2 Warm oil in a large skillet over medium-high heat. Add onion and cook, stirring frequently, until tender and translucent, about 3 minutes. Add garlic and chili powder and cook, stirring, for 1 minute longer. Stir in beans and tomatoes. Cook, stirring, until just warmed through, about 2 minutes. Stir in lemon juice and cilantro. Season with salt and pepper.

3 Spoon bean mixture onto chips. Sprinkle cheese on top. Broil, watching and turning pan often, until nachos are hot and cheese is bubbly, about 1 minute. Top with avocado and yogurt, transfer to a platter and serve.
PER SERVING: 240 Cal., 9g Fat (2g Sat.), 7mg Chol., 6g Fiber, 15g Pro., 26g Carb., 659mg Sod.

Chipotle Potato Salad

Sides

Jicama, Radish and Mango Salad

Kitchen tips

❋ **Switch produce.** Jicama is a crunchy root vegetable popular in Mexican cooking. If you can't find it or don't care for it, use strips of celery instead. You also can substitute diced Granny Smith apple for the mango for a different flavor.

❋ **Wait it out.** For the best texture, don't toss the dressing with the salad until just before serving.

Prep: 30 min.

Serves: 8

Cost per serving:

96¢

- 2 Tbsp. plus 1 tsp. lime juice
- 1 tsp. Dijon mustard
- ¼ tsp. salt
- ⅛ tsp. pepper

- 3 Tbsp. olive oil
- 1 small shallot, minced
- 1 medium jicama (about 1 lb.)
- 8 medium radishes, thinly sliced
- 1 medium ripe but firm mango, diced
- Large Boston lettuce leaves, for serving, optional
- 2 tsp. chopped fresh parsley

1 In a large bowl, whisk together 2 Tbsp. lime juice, mustard, salt and pepper. Whisk in olive oil and shallot.

2 Using a sharp knife, cut ends off jicama and peel by cutting from top to bottom. Cut into matchstick-size pieces and toss jicama with remaining 1 tsp. lime juice.

3 Just before serving, add jicama, radishes and mango to bowl with dressing. Toss well to coat completely. Line a serving platter with lettuce leaves, if desired, and arrange salad in center. Sprinkle with parsley and serve.

PER SERVING: 87 Cal., 5g Fat (1g Sat.), 0mg Chol., 3g Fiber, 1g Pro., 10g Carb., 93mg Sod.

Cucumber Salad

Prep: 15 min.

Serves: 8

Cost per serving:

60¢

- 1 red onion, halved and thinly sliced
- 3 Tbsp. rice vinegar
- 3 cucumbers, peeled, seeded and thinly sliced
- Salt and pepper
- 2 Tbsp. olive oil
- 2 Tbsp. chopped fresh dill

1 Toss onion with 1 Tbsp. rice vinegar and set aside. Place cucumbers in a colander and toss with ¼ tsp. salt. Drain cucumbers for 10 minutes. Pat dry.

2 Mix onion and cucumbers in a large bowl. Toss with olive oil and remaining 2 Tbsp. vinegar. Add dill; season with salt and pepper. Cover and chill until ready to serve.

PER SERVING: 53 Cal., 4g Fat (0g Sat.), 0mg Chol., 1g Fiber, 1g Pro., 5g Carb., 238mg Sod.

Stir-Fried Broccoli

Prep: 10 min.

Cook: 15 min.

Serves: 8

Cost per serving:

90¢

- 2 Tbsp. sesame seeds
- 2 Tbsp. vegetable oil
- 1 Tbsp. sesame oil
- 2 cloves garlic, minced
- ½ red bell pepper, cored, seeded and thinly sliced
- 2 lb. broccoli florets, cut into bite-size pieces (about 12 cups)
- 1 cup low-sodium chicken broth
- Salt and pepper

1 Cook sesame seeds in a small skillet over medium-high heat, stirring constantly, until lightly toasted and beginning to release oil, about 1 minute. Remove sesame seeds to a plate to cool.

2 Warm vegetable oil with sesame oil in a large skillet over medium-high heat. Add garlic and sauté until fragrant, about 1 minute. Add bell pepper and broccoli; stir well until coated in oil. Sauté until broccoli is slightly softened, 2 to 3 minutes.

3 Pour in broth; bring to a simmer. Reduce heat to low, cover and cook, stirring once or twice, until broccoli is tender, about 5 minutes. Sprinkle with sesame seeds. Season with salt and pepper; serve warm.

PER SERVING: 103 Cal., 7g Fat (1g Sat.), 0mg Chol., 3g Fiber, 4g Pro., 7g Carb., 187mg Sod.

Kitchen tip

✳ **Use the whole thing.** Instead of buying a bag of just the florets, save money by purchasing a whole head of broccoli. Peel and slice the tender stem and stir-fry with the florets.

Kitchen tips

Kitchen tips

✳ **Swap herbs.** Fresh herbs are better in this dish, but if you prefer to use dried, toss in 2 tsp. each parsley and basil plus a generous ¼ tsp. oregano.

✳ **Serve it well.** These crowd-pleasing tomatoes make a great accompaniment to grilled steak, pork or chicken.

✳ **Use it up.** Most any bread you have can make good crumbs, including ends of loaves, English muffins or pitas.

Herb-Stuffed Tomatoes

Prep: 30 min.
Bake: 30 min.
Serves: 8
Cost per serving:

$1.64

- 8 tomatoes
- Salt and pepper
- 1 Tbsp. unsalted butter
- ¼ cup olive oil
- ½ onion, finely chopped

- 4 cloves garlic, finely chopped
- 3 cups fresh bread crumbs
- 2 Tbsp. chopped chives
- 2 Tbsp. chopped fresh parsley
- 2 Tbsp. chopped fresh basil
- 1 tsp. dried oregano
- 1 cup grated Parmesan
- 1 large egg, beaten

1 Preheat oven to 375°F. Cut tomatoes in half and spoon out flesh. Put flesh in a sieve set over a bowl and press down to release juices; reserve. Season inside of tomatoes with salt and pepper; invert over a baking sheet lined with a kitchen towel.

2 Melt butter with 2 Tbsp. olive oil in a skillet over low heat. Add onion and sauté for 5 minutes. Add garlic; sauté for 3 minutes. Remove from heat. Stir in bread crumbs, herbs and Parmesan. Stir in ¼ cup reserved tomato juice, then egg.

3 Stuff tomatoes with bread-crumb mixture. Grease a 9-by-13-inch baking dish. Put stuffed tomatoes in dish in a single layer. Drizzle with 2 Tbsp. oil. Bake until top is browned and crisp, about 30 minutes.

PER SERVING: 325 Cal., 15g Fat (5g Sat.), 41mg Chol., 4g Fiber, 12g Pro., 36g Carb., 649mg Sod.

English Roast Potatoes

Prep: 15 min.

Cook: 1 hr.

Serves: 8

Cost per serving:

44¢

- **8 Tbsp. solid vegetable shortening, cut into pieces**
- **4 lb. large russet potatoes, peeled and cut into large chunks**
- **Salt and pepper**

1 Preheat oven to 375°F. Bring a large pot of water to a boil.

2 Put shortening in a large, shallow baking dish and place on top rack of oven as oven heats. In a large pot, cover potatoes with boiling water, add 1 tsp. salt and simmer over low heat for 10 minutes. Drain potatoes and return to pot. Cover pot and, wearing oven mitts, hold lid on firmly and shake pot up and down 2 or 3 times to roughen edges of potatoes.

3 Remove baking dish from oven and place over 2 burners on medium-high heat. Carefully transfer potatoes to baking dish and baste them with melted shortening. Return baking dish to oven and roast potatoes for 30 minutes, basting once during roasting.

4 Raise temperature of oven to 425°F. Using tongs, turn over potatoes and continue to cook until golden brown and crispy, 20 to 30 minutes longer, turning them halfway through so that all sides get crispy and brown.

Remove potatoes from shortening, allow to drain on paper towels, season with salt and pepper and serve immediately.

PER SERVING: 290 Cal., 12g Fat (3g Sat.), 0mg Chol., 3g Fiber, 5g Pro., 41g Carb., 157mg Sod.

Kitchen tip

✳ **Dress it up.**
Sprinkle on chopped fresh parsley, thyme or chives just before serving to give the potatoes a pretty shot of green.

Oaxacan Grilled Corn

Prep: 15 min.

Soak: 30 min.

Cook: 25 min.

Serves: 8

Cost per serving:

60¢

- **8 ears fresh corn, with husks**
- **3 Tbsp. unsalted butter, melted**
- **⅔ cup mayonnaise**
- **1 Tbsp. chili powder**
- **½ cup grated Parmesan**
- **2 limes, cut into wedges**
- **Salt and pepper**

1. Pull down corn husks and remove silks. Place husks back over corn and soak in large bowls filled with cold water for 30 minutes.

2. Preheat a gas grill to medium. Drain corn on paper towels and pat dry. Pull down husks and brush kernels evenly with melted butter. Place husks back over corn and tie ends with kitchen twine to keep in place. Arrange corn flat on grill with string ends away from direct heat and cook, turning often, until tender, 20 to 25 minutes.

3. Cut away twine and pull down husks.

Spread mayonnaise over each ear, then sprinkle generously with chili powder and Parmesan. Serve with lime wedges and salt and pepper for seasoning.

PER SERVING: 279 Cal., 22g Fat (7g Sat.), 30mg Chol., 3g Fiber, 5g Pro., 18g Carb., 372mg Sod.

Kitchen tips

✳ **Hold on.** Leave a couple of inches of stalk on the end of each ear of corn to make a good handle. Pull off a piece of the husk and use it to tie up the rest decoratively, as shown at right.

✳ **Be prepared.** This corn is delicious, but it's messy to eat, so have some damp paper towels or wipes handy.

✳ **Add flavor.** Stir a little chopped fresh cilantro into the mayonnaise.

Green Beans with Shallots and Almonds

Prep: 15 min.

Cook: 15 min.

Serves: 8

Cost per serving:

$1.03

- **Salt**
- **2 lb. green beans, cut into 1-inch pieces**
- **2 Tbsp. olive oil**
- **2 cups sliced shallots (about 4 large)**
- **2 Tbsp. unsalted butter, at room temperature**
- **½ cup sliced almonds, toasted**

1. Fill a large bowl with ice cubes and water. Bring a large pot of salted water to a boil.

Add green beans to pot and cook until crisp-tender, about 5 minutes. Drain and plunge beans into ice bath to stop cooking. Drain beans again and dry on paper towels.

2. Warm olive oil in a large skillet over medium heat. Add shallots, then sauté until softened and lightly browned, about 7 minutes. Add green beans and butter; sauté until green beans are heated through, about 2 minutes. Sprinkle with toasted almonds and serve.

PER SERVING: 150 Cal., 10g Fat (3g Sat.), 8mg Chol., 4g Fiber, 4g Pro., 14g Carb., 164mg Sod.

*Oaxacan
Grilled Corn*

Bean, Corn and Cherry Tomato Salad

Prep: 15 min.

Serves: 8

Cost per serving:

$1.08

- 3 Tbsp. red wine vinegar
- 3 Tbsp. olive oil
- 2 15.5-oz. cans black beans, drained and rinsed
- 3 cups fresh corn kernels (or frozen, thawed)
- 12 cherry tomatoes, halved or quartered
- 2 Tbsp. lemon juice
- 1 avocado, peeled, pitted and cut into cubes
- Salt and pepper

1 In a large bowl, whisk vinegar with oil until blended. Add beans, corn and tomatoes.

2 In a small bowl, toss lemon juice and avocado. Add to bean mixture.

3 Just before serving, stir salad; season with salt and pepper. Serve at room temperature, or cover and refrigerate to serve cold later.

PER SERVING: 197 Cal., 9g Fat (1g Sat.), 0mg Chol., 9g Fiber, 7g Pro., 29g Carb., 574mg Sod.

Asparagus and Radish Sauté

Prep: 30 min.

Cook: 14 min.

Serves: 8

Cost per serving:

$1.45

- 1 Tbsp. extra-virgin olive oil
- 5 large shallots, sliced thinly lengthwise through the root
- 2 lb. fresh asparagus, ends trimmed, cut on diagonal into 2-inch pieces
- 1 bunch small radishes (about 8 oz.), trimmed, thinly sliced
- 1 packed tsp. finely grated lemon zest
- 1 Tbsp. unsalted butter
- Salt and pepper
- Juice of ½ lemon

1 Warm oil in a large nonstick skillet over medium-high heat. Add shallots and cook, stirring frequently, until wilted, about 5 minutes. Add asparagus to skillet and continue to cook, tossing frequently, until asparagus is crisp-tender, 5 to 7 minutes longer.

2 Add radishes, lemon zest and butter to skillet and season with salt and pepper. Cook, stirring often, until radishes are just warmed through, about 1 minute. Sprinkle lemon juice over vegetable mixture and toss again. Season with additional salt and pepper, if desired. Serve immediately.

PER SERVING: 68 Cal., 3g Fat (1g Sat.), 4mg Chol., 3g Fiber, 3g Pro., 9g Carb., 161mg Sod.

Jalapeño and Lime Refried Beans

Prep: 30 min.
Soak: 8 hr.
Cook: 6 hr. 10 min.
Serves: 8
Cost per serving:

36¢

- 3 cups dried pinto beans, soaked 8 hr. or overnight in cold water
- 1 medium onion, quartered
- 5 cloves garlic (3 crushed, 2 minced)
- 3 Tbsp. vegetable oil
- 1 medium jalapeño, stemmed, seeded and minced
- 3 Tbsp. fresh lime juice
- 3 tsp. grated lime zest
- Salt and pepper
- Queso fresco and chopped cilantro, for serving, optional

1 Drain beans; place in slow cooker. Add onion and crushed garlic. Pour in enough water to cover. Cook, covered, until beans are tender, about 4 hours on high or 6 on low.

2 Drain cooked beans, reserving liquid. Use a potato masher, pastry blender or fork to work bean mixture into a thick mass.

3 Warm oil in a large pot over medium-high heat. Add minced garlic and jalapeño. Cook, stirring often, until softened, 3 to 5 minutes. Stir in mashed bean mixture and cook until warmed through, about 5 minutes. Add small amounts of reserved cooking liquid to thin as desired. Mixture should have the consistency of thick mashed potatoes.

4 Remove pot from heat and stir in lime juice and zest. Season generously with salt and pepper. Top with queso fresco and chopped cilantro, if desired.

PER SERVING: 283 Cal., 5g Fat (0g Sat.), 0mg Chol., 15g Fiber, 14g Pro., 43g Carb., 146mg Sod.

ANDREW McCAUL, FOOD STYLING: LYNN MILLER

Cheesy Potato Gratin

additional salt and pepper.

3 Bring milk to a boil over medium-high heat. Pour milk over potatoes. Cover dish with foil and bake until potatoes are tender, about 45 minutes. (Don't worry if mixture looks curdled at this point.) Remove foil, sprinkle remaining cheese mixture on top and bake, uncovered, until potatoes are very tender and top of gratin is golden brown and bubbling, about 45 minutes longer. Let stand for 10 minutes before serving.

PER SERVING: 404 Cal., 17g Fat (10g Sat.), 55mg Chol., 3g Fiber, 16g Pro., 49g Carb., 393mg Sod.

Prep: 35 min.
Bake: 1 hr. 30 min.
Serves: 8
Cost per serving:

$1.03

- ¾ cup shredded sharp Cheddar
- ¾ cup shredded Swiss cheese
- ½ cup grated Parmesan

- 3 Tbsp. all-purpose flour
- 4 lb. russet potatoes, peeled, sliced crosswise ¼-inch thick
- Salt and pepper
- 4 Tbsp. unsalted butter, softened
- 3 cups whole milk

1 Preheat oven to 375°F. Butter a 9-by-13-inch baking dish and place on a baking sheet lined with foil.

2 Combine all cheeses in a large bowl. Sprinkle flour on top of cheese mixture and toss to coat. Arrange ½ of potatoes, overlapping, on bottom of baking dish. Season with ¾ tsp. salt and ¼ tsp. pepper. Dot with ½ of butter. Sprinkle ½ of cheese mixture on top. Cover with remaining potatoes and dot with remaining butter. Season with

Kitchen tips

✳ **Swap spuds.** You can use another type of potato for this dish. Red potatoes and Yukon gold work equally well. Sizes vary, so purchase by weight.

✳ **Prevent sticking.** Lightly mist one side of foil with cooking spray and place it spray-side down when covering the baking dish.

Kitchen tips

✳ **Plan wisely.** This salad tastes best the day it's made. For maximum flavor, don't refrigerate before serving.

✳ **Swap onions.** You may substitute half of a finely chopped sweet onion for the scallions, if you like. Look for a variety such as Vidalia, Walla Walla or Maui.

Chipotle Potato Salad

Prep: 10 min.
Cook: 20 min.
Serves: 6
Cost per serving:

70¢

- 2 lb. small red potatoes
- Salt and pepper
- 2 Tbsp. red wine vinegar

- 2 ribs celery, finely chopped (about ½ cup)
- 3 scallions, white and light green parts only, finely chopped
- 1 Tbsp. minced seeded chipotle chiles in adobo sauce
- ½ cup finely chopped fresh parsley
- 3 Tbsp. olive oil

1 Place potatoes in a large pot and cover with water. Add 1 Tbsp. salt, bring to a boil over high heat and cook until potatoes are tender, about 10 minutes (poke with tip of a knife to check). Drain potatoes and let stand just until cool enough to handle. Cut each potato into quarters and transfer to a large bowl.

2 Sprinkle potatoes with red wine vinegar and let stand 10 minutes. Add celery, scallions, chipotles and parsley to bowl; stir to combine. Drizzle potato salad with olive oil, season with salt and pepper and mix thoroughly. Serve at room temperature.
PER SERVING: 202 Cal., 7g Fat (1g Sat.), 0mg Chol., 3g Fiber, 4g Pro., 31g Carb., 234mg Sod.

Scalloped Potatoes

Scalloped Potatoes

Prep: 10 min.
Bake: 55 min.
Serves: 8
Cost per serving:

97¢

- 1 large onion, halved and thinly sliced
- 2½ lb. red potatoes, peeled and sliced ⅛-inch thick
- 1 tsp. salt
- 1 tsp. pepper
- 1 cup shredded Gruyère
- 4 Tbsp. unsalted butter, melted
- 1¼ cups milk

1 Preheat oven to 425°F. Grease a 9-inch round baking dish.

2 Arrange ½ of onion slices in a circular pattern in dish, overlapping slightly. Top with a third of potato slices, then sprinkle with ½ tsp. salt, ½ tsp. pepper and ½ cup shredded Gruyère. Drizzle with 2 Tbsp. melted butter. Repeat layers and add a top layer of potato slices.

3 Bring milk to a boil and pour over potato slices in baking dish. Bake until tender and golden, 45 to 55 minutes.

PER SERVING: 241 Cal., 12g Fat (7g Sat.), 36mg Chol., 3g Fiber, 8g Pro., 27g Carb., 366mg Sod.

Green Salad with Roasted Beets, Goat Cheese and Almonds

Prep: 15 min.
Cook: 1 hr.
Serves: 8
Cost per serving:

$1.65

- 4 medium beets
- 2 Tbsp. unsalted butter
- ½ cup sliced almonds
- Salt and pepper
- 2 Tbsp. red wine vinegar
- 1 Tbsp. lemon juice
- 1 tsp. Dijon mustard
- 2 Tbsp. vegetable oil
- 2 Tbsp. olive oil
- 10 cups torn assorted lettuce greens such as red- and green-leaf, romaine, arugula, Boston and radicchio
- ½ cup fresh goat cheese, crumbled

1 Preheat oven to 425°F. Trim beets and place on a large piece of aluminum foil. Tightly crimp foil to seal and roast until beets are tender, about 1 hour. Cool, peel and cut into 1-inch dice.

2 Melt butter in a small skillet over medium-high heat. Add almonds, lower heat to medium and cook, stirring often, until light golden brown, about 3 minutes. Drain almonds on paper towels and season with salt and pepper.

3 Combine vinegar, lemon juice and mustard in a large bowl. Whisk until blended and smooth. Whisk in both oils; season with salt and pepper. Pile lettuce on dressing and toss to coat. Toss in beets and sprinkle with goat cheese and almonds. Serve cold.

PER SERVING: 174 Cal., 15g Fat (4g Sat.), 13mg Chol., 3g Fiber, 4g Pro., 7g Carb., 235mg Sod.

Butterscotch Pudding Pie

Desserts

Apple Crepes

Prep: 10 min.
Stand: 30 min.
Cook: 40 min.
Serves: 6
Cost per serving:

60¢

- 1¼ cups all-purpose flour
- Pinch of salt
- ¼ cup sugar
- 1¼ cups low-fat milk

- 4 large eggs, lightly beaten
- 1 Tbsp. unsalted butter
- 3 tart apples such as Granny Smith, peeled, cut into ½-inch cubes
- ¼ tsp. cinnamon
- ¼ cup apple juice or cider
- Plain or vanilla yogurt, optional

1 Make crepe batter: In a blender, pulse flour, salt and 1 Tbsp. sugar. Add milk and eggs and blend until mixture is thick and no lumps remain. Pour into a bowl and let stand at room temperature for 30 minutes.

2 Make filling: Melt butter in a skillet and add apples. Cook, stirring occasionally, until apples begin to soften, about 3 minutes. Sprinkle with cinnamon and remaining sugar; sauté until apples begin to brown, about 5 minutes longer. Pour in juice and cook 2 minutes longer, stirring. Remove from heat.

3 Whisk batter. If necessary, thin with an additional 1 Tbsp. milk (crepe batter should have consistency of thin cream). Mist a 10-inch nonstick skillet with cooking spray; warm over medium heat. Ladle ¼ cup batter into skillet. Quickly tilt skillet so batter coats surface in a thin layer. Cook until edges of crepe begin to brown, about 2 minutes. Lift edge of crepe and, using your fingers, carefully flip. Cook for 30 seconds; transfer to a plate. Cover with a clean kitchen towel. Repeat with remaining batter, misting skillet with cooking spray between crepes as necessary.

4 Rewarm apple mixture. Fold each crepe into quarters. Arrange 2 crepes on each plate; top with apple mixture and a dollop of yogurt, if desired.

PER SERVING: 251 Cal., 6g Fat (3g Sat.), 148mg Chol., 1g Fiber, 9g Pro., 41g Carb., 101mg Sod.

Kitchen tip

✳ **Make a switch.**
Don't have buttermilk
on hand? Use low-fat
plain yogurt instead.

Cocoa Cupcakes

Prep: 10 min.
Bake: 20 min.
Serves: 12
Cost per serving:

30¢

- 1 cup all-purpose flour
- ½ cup unsweetened cocoa powder
- 1 tsp. baking soda
- ⅛ tsp. salt
- 2 large eggs, separated

- 4 Tbsp. unsalted butter, at room temperature
- ½ cup sugar
- 1 tsp. vanilla extract
- ½ cup low-fat buttermilk
- ¼ cup miniature chocolate chips
- 2 Tbsp. confectioners' sugar, optional

1 Preheat oven to 350°F. Line a 12-cup muffin tin with paper liners. In a bowl, sift flour, cocoa, baking soda and salt.

2 Using an electric mixer on high speed, beat egg whites in a clean, dry bowl until stiff peaks form. Rinse and dry beaters. In a separate bowl, beat butter and sugar until light. Add yolks, one at a time, beating well after each. Beat in vanilla. With mixer on medium-low speed, beat in ⅓ of flour mixture, then ½ of buttermilk. Repeat, ending with flour.

3 Fold in ⅓ of egg whites, then fold in remaining whites and chocolate chips.

4 Divide batter evenly among muffin cups. Bake until a toothpick inserted into a cupcake comes out clean, 18 to 20 minutes. Let cool in muffin tin on a wire rack for 5 minutes, then remove cupcakes to rack to cool completely. Sift confectioners' sugar over cupcakes, if desired.

PER SERVING (1 CUPCAKE):
158 Cal., 7g Fat (4g Sat.),
47mg Chol., 1g Fiber, 4g Pro.,
22g Carb., 156mg Sod.

Key Lime Bars

Prep: 10 min.
Bake: 55 min.
Chill: 1 hr.
Yield: 12 bars
Cost per serving:

22¢

CRUST:
- 8 Tbsp. (1 stick) unsalted butter, softened
- ¼ cup sugar
- 1 cup all-purpose flour
- ¼ tsp. salt

FILLING:
- 2 large eggs
- 1 large egg yolk
- 1 cup sugar
- ⅓ cup Key lime juice
- 1 tsp. grated lime zest
- 2 Tbsp. all-purpose flour
- Confectioners' sugar, for dusting, optional

1 Preheat oven to 350°F. Line an 8-inch baking pan with foil, leaving a 2-inch overhang. Mist foil with cooking spray.

2 Make crust: Using an electric mixer on medium-high speed, beat together butter and sugar until light, about 2 minutes. Add flour and salt and beat until just blended. Press crust evenly over bottom of prepared pan. Bake until firm and light golden around edges, 20 to 25 minutes. Let cool slightly on a rack.

3 Make filling: Using an electric mixer on medium speed, beat eggs, yolk and sugar until smooth. Stir in Key lime juice and lime zest. Fold in flour until just combined. Pour filling over crust. Bake until set, 20 to 30 minutes. Cool on a wire rack. Cover; refrigerate for at least 1 hour or overnight. Use foil overhang to remove bars from pan to cut. Dust with confectioners' sugar just before serving, if desired.

PER SERVING (1 BAR):
210 Cal., 9g Fat (5g Sat.), 73mg Chol., 0g Fiber, 3g Pro., 30g Carb., 62mg Sod.

Peach-Berry Crumble

Prep: 30 min.
Bake: 55 min.
Serves: 8
Cost per serving:
$1.61

TOPPING:
- **1 cup quick-cooking oats**
- **½ cup all-purpose flour**
- **½ cup packed dark brown sugar**
- **1 tsp. cinnamon**
- **½ tsp. salt**
- **8 Tbsp. (1 stick) unsalted butter, melted**
- **¼ cup sliced almonds**

FILLING:
- **1½ lb. firm, ripe peaches (4 or 5)**
- **½ cup sugar**
- **¼ cup all-purpose flour**
- **Pinch of salt**
- **1 cup fresh blueberries**
- **1 cup fresh raspberries**

1 Preheat oven to 350°F. Lightly butter a 9-inch pie plate. Line a large, rimmed baking sheet with foil. Make topping: In a bowl, mix oats, flour, brown sugar, cinnamon and salt. Stir in butter until crumbly. Toss in nuts.

2 Make filling: Bring a large pot of water to a boil; have ready a large bowl filled with ice water. Using a sharp knife, cut a shallow X into bottom of peaches. Blanch peaches until skins begin to wrinkle, 30 to 60 seconds. Remove with a slotted spoon and place in ice water to cool. Using your fingers, slip off skins; cut peaches in half, remove pits and slice fruit into wedges.

3 In a bowl, toss peaches with sugar, flour and salt. Fold in berries. Let stand for 5 minutes. Transfer to prepared pie plate. Sprinkle with topping, place on prepared baking sheet and bake until filling bubbles and topping is golden, 50 to 55 minutes. Let cool on a wire rack. Serve warm or at room temperature, with vanilla ice cream, if desired.

PER SERVING: 389 Cal., 15g Fat (8g Sat.), 30mg Chol., 6g Fiber, 6g Pro., 61g Carb., 226mg Sod.

Mixed-Berry Pretzel Tart

Prep: 20 min.
Cook: 8 min.
Chill: 4 hr.
Serves: 12
Cost per serving:

$1.49

CRUST:
- 2 cups crushed pretzels
- 3 Tbsp. sugar
- 12 Tbsp. (1½ sticks) unsalted butter, melted

FILLING:
- 8 oz. cream cheese
- ¾ cup plus 1 Tbsp. sugar
- 7 oz. plain Greek yogurt (not fat-free)
- 2 tsp. vanilla extract
- 2 3-oz. packages strawberry gelatin
- 1 16-oz. package frozen unsweetened sliced strawberries
- 1 16-oz. package frozen unsweetened blueberries
- ¾ cup heavy cream

1 Make crust: Preheat oven to 400°F; mist a 9-by-13-inch baking dish with cooking spray. Pulse pretzels, sugar and butter in food processor to combine. Press mixture into dish and bake for 8 minutes. Transfer to a wire rack; let cool completely.

2 Make filling: Using an electric mixer on medium speed, beat cream cheese and ¾ cup sugar for 2 minutes. Fold in yogurt and vanilla. Spread over crust. Cover; chill for at least 2 hours.

3 In a bowl, dissolve gelatin in 2 cups boiling water. Let cool for 15 minutes. Stir in berries and pour over cream cheese layer. Chill until firm, 2 to 3 hours.

4 Whip cream until soft peaks form. Add remaining 1 Tbsp. sugar; whip until stiff peaks form. Serve tart with whipped cream.
PER SERVING: 411 Cal., 26g Fat (16g Sat.), 76mg Chol., 2g Fiber, 11g Pro., 32g Carb., 526mg Sod.

"Fried" Ice Cream Truffles

Prep: 25 min.
Bake: 10 min.
Stand: 30 min.
Freeze: 30 min.
Yield: 16 truffles
Cost per serving:

43¢

- 2 Tbsp. unsalted butter
- 2 Tbsp. sugar
- ½ tsp. cinnamon
- 1 cup sliced almonds
- 1 quart vanilla or dulce de leche ice cream
- 1 cup frosted cornflakes
- ½ tsp. salt

1 Preheat oven to 350°F; line a baking sheet with parchment. Place butter, sugar and cinnamon in a bowl and microwave on high until butter has melted, about 1 minute. Stir to combine. Place almonds in a bowl and toss with butter mixture. Spread almonds on prepared baking sheet. Bake for 10 minutes, stirring halfway through. Let cool on sheet on a wire rack for 30 minutes.

2 Line a baking sheet with parchment; place in freezer. Let ice cream stand at room temperature for 15 minutes to soften. Pulse almond mixture, cornflakes and salt in food processor until mixture resembles coarse crumbs. Transfer to a shallow dish.

3 Scoop ice cream into balls using a 1¼-inch scoop. Roll in almond mixture, gently pressing to adhere. Arrange on sheet in freezer. Freeze for at least 30 minutes or up to 24 hours.
PER SERVING (1 TRUFFLE): 197 Cal., 13g Fat (7g Sat.), 64mg Chol., 1g Fiber, 4g Pro., 16g Carb., 122mg Sod.

Mixed-Berry Pretzel Tart

Rosé-Poached Pears

Prep: 10 min.
Cook: 50 min.
Serves: 4
Cost per serving:

$4.22

- 1 750ml bottle dry rosé wine
- ½ cup sugar
- 1 2-inch piece lemon zest
- 1 3-inch cinnamon stick, broken in half
- 1 tsp. vanilla extract
- 4 large ripe but firm Bosc pears (about 2 lb. total)

1 Combine wine, sugar, lemon zest, cinnamon stick and vanilla in a wide saucepan. Bring to a boil over high heat, stirring just until sugar has dissolved. Reduce heat to medium and simmer for 2 minutes to blend flavors.

2 Peel pears and cut in half lengthwise.

Use a small spoon or a melon baller to scoop out center core and seeds. Working quickly, gently lower pears into poaching liquid. Simmer, gently turning over pears with a large spoon every 5 minutes, until pears are tender when pierced with a knife, 15 to 25 minutes, depending on ripeness. (Work in batches, if necessary.) Use a slotted spoon to transfer pears to a large bowl.

3 Raise heat to high and bring poaching liquid back to a boil. Boil rapidly until poaching liquid has reduced and thickened slightly, 20 to 25 minutes. Let liquid cool slightly, remove cinnamon stick and pour liquid over pears. Serve warm or cover, refrigerate and serve chilled.

PER SERVING: 348 Cal., 0g Fat (0g Sat.), 0mg Chol., 7g Fiber, 1g Pro., 59g Carb., 9mg Sod.

Strawberry-Rhubarb Crumble Pie

baking sheet with foil.

2 Prepare filling: Mix all filling ingredients in a large bowl and let rest for 15 minutes, stirring occasionally.

3 Make topping: Mix flour, sugar and salt in a bowl. Using your fingers, rub in butter until mixture forms clumps. Stir in almonds.

4 Spoon filling into pie crust; sprinkle evenly with topping. Place pie on lined baking sheet; bake 15 minutes. Turn oven down to 350°F and bake until filling is bubbly and topping is brown and crisp, about 1 hour longer. Let cool on a wire rack for at least 20 minutes before serving.

PER SERVING: 696 Cal., 19g Fat (6g Sat.), 13mg Chol., 4g Fiber, 4g Pro., 133g Carb., 129mg Sod.

Prep: 30 min.
Stand: 15 min.
Bake: 1 hr. 15 min.
Serves: 8
Cost per serving:

$1.97

- 1 9-inch unbaked pie crust (homemade or store-bought)

FILLING:
- 4 cups rhubarb, sliced ¼-inch thick
- 4 cups strawberries, each cut in half
- 1 Tbsp. grated orange zest
- 1½ cups sugar
- ½ cup instant tapioca

TOPPING:
- 1 cup all-purpose flour
- ½ cup packed light brown sugar
- ⅛ tsp. salt
- 8 Tbsp. (1 stick) unsalted butter, softened
- ⅓ cup sliced almonds

1 Preheat oven to 425°F. Place a rack in lower third of oven and line a

Kitchen tip

✳ **Omit the nuts.** If you don't care for almonds or you have an allergy, swap in the same amount of rolled oats (don't use instant).

RYAN BENYI, FOOD STYLING: STEPHANA BOTTOM

Cappuccino Bundt Cake

Prep: 20 min.
Bake: 33 min.
Serves: 12
Cost per serving:

57¢

CAKE:
- **2 cups all-purpose flour**
- **1 tsp. baking soda**
- **1¾ cups sugar**
- **½ tsp. salt**
- **½ cup vegetable oil**
- **8 Tbsp. unsalted butter**
- **2 Tbsp. plus ¼ tsp. unsweetened cocoa**
- **3 Tbsp. plus ¼ tsp. instant espresso powder**
- **2 Tbsp. plus ¼ tsp. cinnamon**
- **2 large eggs, lightly beaten, at room temperature**
- **½ cup sour cream, at room temperature**
- **1 tsp. vanilla extract**

GLAZE:
- **4 oz. white chocolate, chopped**
- **1 Tbsp. unsalted butter**
- **1 cup confectioners' sugar**
- **3 Tbsp. whole milk**

1 Preheat oven to 375°F. Grease and flour a 12-cup Bundt cake pan.

2 In a bowl, whisk flour, baking soda, sugar and salt. In a saucepan, whisk oil, butter, 2 Tbsp. cocoa, 3 Tbsp. espresso powder, 2 Tbsp. cinnamon and 1 cup water. Bring to a simmer over medium-low heat, stirring. In a bowl, whisk eggs, sour cream and vanilla.

3 Stir cocoa mixture into flour mixture. Fold in egg mixture. Pour into Bundt pan, smoothing top. Bake until a skewer inserted in center comes out clean, 25 to 33 minutes. Let cool on a rack for 10 minutes. Remove from pan; let cool completely.

4 In a small bowl, whisk ¼ tsp. each cocoa, espresso powder and cinnamon.

5 Make glaze: In a heatproof bowl set over 1 inch of simmering water, melt chocolate with butter. Remove from heat and let cool. In a bowl, whisk confectioners' sugar and milk. Stir in chocolate mixture. Drizzle glaze over cake. Sift cocoa mixture over top; let stand until glaze has set.
PER SERVING: 479 Cal., 24g Fat (10g Sat.), 64mg Chol., 2g Fiber, 5g Pro., 63g Carb., 231mg Sod.

Frozen Banana "Custard" with Warm Chocolate Sauce

Prep: 5 min.

Serves: 4

Cost per serving:

78¢

- **4 oz. semisweet chocolate chips**
- **5 ripe bananas, peeled and cut into small pieces, frozen**
- **¼ cup milk**
- **½ tsp. vanilla extract**

1 In a microwave-safe bowl, combine chocolate chips and 3 Tbsp. water; microwave on high until just melted, 1 to 1½ minutes. Whisk until smooth.

2 Place bananas in a food processor and pulse until broken down. Add milk and vanilla and process until smooth, scraping down sides of bowl once or twice as necessary.

3 Scoop banana puree into 4 dishes and top with warm chocolate sauce. Serve immediately.

PER SERVING: 276 Cal., 9g Fat (6g Sat.), 2mg Chol., 6g Fiber, 3g Pro., 52g Carb., 13mg Sod.

Kitchen tips

✳ **Add crunch.** Toss chopped toasted pecans, walnuts or almonds—or some toasted coconut—on top.

✳ **Be a cutup.** Slice the bananas into small pieces before freezing them, so they're easier to puree. Place the pieces in a ziplock bag and freeze. Mark the bag with the date and contents (the bananas will keep for 6 months). Freeze extras for muffins or smoothies.

✳ **Hold off.** Wait until your bananas are very ripe (there should be brown specks on the peels) before slicing and freezing them. They're much sweeter.

✳ **Swap chocolates.** For a stronger flavor, use bittersweet chocolate instead of semisweet. Stir in a pinch of instant coffee granules for a deeper flavor—you won't taste the coffee, but it adds richness.

Marshmallow-Topped Chocolate Pudding Cakes

Marshmallow-Topped Chocolate Pudding Cakes

Prep: 15 min.
Bake: 18 min.
Serves: 4
Cost per serving:

$1.24

- 4 Tbsp. unsalted butter
- 5 oz. bittersweet chocolate, chopped
- 1½ Tbsp. all-purpose flour
- ¼ cup packed light brown sugar
- 2 large eggs
- 1 tsp. vanilla extract
- ¼ tsp. salt
- 4 marshmallows

1 Preheat oven to 375°F. Mist 4 6-oz. ramekins with cooking spray and place on a baking sheet.

2 Combine butter and chocolate in a large bowl; microwave on high until almost melted, 1 to 2 minutes. Stir until smooth; let cool. Stir in flour.

3 With an electric mixer on medium-high speed, beat sugar, eggs, vanilla and salt until lightened, about 5 minutes. Fold in chocolate mixture.

4 Divide batter among ramekins; bake until pudding cakes have risen and are cracked on top but still wet in center, 12 to 15 minutes. Press a marshmallow on top of each; bake until marshmallows have melted and begin to brown, 2 to 3 minutes. Let cool on a wire rack for 5 minutes; serve.

PER SERVING: 397 Cal., 29g Fat (16g Sat.), 136mg Chol., 3g Fiber, 6g Pro., 38g Carb., 188mg Sod.

Mocha Truffle Cake

Prep: 15 min.
Bake: 1 hr.
Stand: 35 min.
Chill: 2 hr.
Serves: 12
Cost per serving:

66¢

- 12 oz. semisweet chocolate, chopped
- 1½ cups sugar
- 1 Tbsp. instant espresso powder
- 12 Tbsp. (1½ sticks) unsalted butter, at room temperature
- 6 large eggs
- 1 tsp. vanilla extract
- 1 Tbsp. confectioners' sugar

1 Preheat oven to 350°F. Butter a 9-inch springform pan and line bottom with parchment. Butter parchment.

2 Process chocolate, sugar and espresso powder in a food processor until chocolate is finely ground, about 30 seconds. With blades in motion, pour in ¾ cup boiling water. Process until chocolate has melted, about 20 seconds. Add butter, eggs and vanilla. Pulse to mix into a thin batter.

3 Pour batter into pan; spread evenly. Bake until set in center, 55 to 60 minutes (cake will appear dry on top and slightly cracked around the edges). Let stand in pan on a wire

rack for 20 minutes; cake may sink in center. Run a knife around edges of pan, remove cake, cover and refrigerate at least 2 hours or overnight.

4 Place cake on a serving plate and let stand for 15 to 30 minutes. Before serving, sift confectioners' sugar on top. Serve with whipped cream, if desired.

PER SERVING: 373 Cal., 22g Fat (13g Sat.), 136mg Chol., 2g Fiber, 5g Pro., 44g Carb., 40mg Sod.

Butterscotch Pudding Pie

Prep: 20 min.
Cook: 1 hr. 20 min.
Chill: 9 hr.
Serves: 10
Cost per serving:

96¢

PUDDING:
- 4 Tbsp. unsalted butter
- 1 cup packed dark brown sugar
- ½ tsp. salt
- ¼ cup plus 2 Tbsp. cornstarch
- 2½ cups whole milk
- 3 large egg yolks
- 2 tsp. whiskey
- 1 tsp. vanilla extract

PIE:
- 1 9-inch pie crust

(homemade or store-bought)
- ¼ cup finely chopped semisweet chocolate
- 1½ cups heavy cream
- 2 Tbsp. sugar
- 1 tsp. vanilla extract
- 1 1.4-oz. Heath candy bar, finely chopped

1 Make pudding: Melt butter in a pan over medium heat. Stir in brown sugar and salt; cook, stirring constantly, for 3 minutes. Remove from heat. In a bowl, whisk cornstarch and ½ cup milk until smooth. Whisk in yolks.

2 Whisk remaining milk into brown sugar mixture, then whisk in cornstarch mixture. Return pan to medium heat and bring to a boil, whisking often. Reduce heat to low; simmer, whisking constantly, until pudding thickens slightly, about 1 minute (it will thicken more as it chills). Remove from heat and stir in whiskey and vanilla. Transfer to bowl and cover with plastic wrap, pressing wrap directly onto surface of pudding. Chill at least 8 hours.

3 Make pie: Preheat oven to 375°F. Line interior of pie crust with parchment. Fill pie crust with dried beans or pie weights, pushing beans or weights up against sides of parchment. Bake for 20 minutes. Remove parchment and weights, prick crust all over with a fork and bake until crust is deep golden brown, 10 to 15 minutes longer. Sprinkle chocolate in crust, let melt, then spread in a thin layer. Transfer to a rack and let cool completely.

4 Using an electric mixer at medium speed, beat cream with sugar and vanilla until mixture holds stiff peaks. Spoon pudding into crust; top with whipped cream. Garnish pie with Heath bar pieces. Refrigerate for 1 hour before serving.

PER SERVING: 437 Cal., 27g Fat (15g Sat.), 134mg Chol., 1g Fiber, 5g Pro., 44g Carb., 266mg Sod.

Cream Cheese Swirl Brownies

Prep: 20 min.
Bake: 45 min.
Stand: 1 hr.
Yield: 16 brownies
Cost per serving:

39¢

SWIRL:
- **4 oz. cream cheese, at room temperature**
- **2 Tbsp. unsalted butter, at room temperature**
- **1 large egg**
- **¼ cup sugar**
- **2 Tbsp. all-purpose flour**
- **1 tsp. vanilla extract**

BROWNIES:
- **8 Tbsp. unsalted butter**
- **4 oz. unsweetened chocolate**
- **1 cup sugar**
- **1 tsp. vanilla extract**
- **⅛ tsp. salt**
- **2 large eggs**
- **½ cup all-purpose flour**

1 Preheat oven to 350°F. Line an 8-inch baking pan with foil, leaving an overhang of at least 2 inches on 2 sides. Mist foil with cooking spray.

2 Make swirl: Using an electric mixer on medium speed, beat cream cheese and butter until creamy and smooth. Add egg and beat until smooth. Beat in sugar, flour and vanilla until combined.

3 Make brownies: Place butter and chocolate in a bowl set over a pan of simmering water (do not let water boil or let bottom of bowl touch water) and melt, stirring often. Remove from heat and stir in sugar, vanilla and salt. Set aside and let cool slightly.

4 Using a mixer on medium-low speed, beat eggs into chocolate mixture one at a time. Gently stir in flour.

5 Spread half of batter in baking pan and carefully spread swirl mixture over brownie batter. Spoon remaining brownie batter on top. Use a knife tip to gently swirl through batters, forming a marble pattern (take care not to scrape pan).

6 Bake brownies until a toothpick inserted into center comes out clean, 40 to 45 minutes. Let cool in pan on a wire rack for at least 1 hour. Use foil overhang to remove brownies from pan; cut into squares.

PER SERVING (1 BROWNIE):
217 Cal., 14g Fat (9g Sat.), 67mg Chol., 1g Fiber, 3g Pro., 22g Carb., 55mg Sod.

Cookies-and-Cream Pudding Parfaits

Prep: 10 min.
Cook: 10 min.
Chill: 1 hr. 30 min.
Serves: 4
Cost per serving:

74¢

- 2 cups whole milk
- ½ cup sugar
- ½ cup heavy cream
- 1 large egg
- 3 Tbsp. cornstarch
- 2 tsp. vanilla extract
- 1 Tbsp. unsalted butter

- 1 cup chopped chocolate-sandwich cookies (about 8 cookies)

1 In a medium saucepan, warm milk and sugar over medium heat (do not let mixture boil), stirring until sugar dissolves. In a small bowl, whisk together cream, egg and cornstarch. Slowly pour cream mixture into warm milk, whisking constantly.

2 Cook, whisking constantly, until mixture is thick enough to coat back of a spoon, 4 to 6 minutes. Remove from heat and add vanilla and butter, stirring until butter melts. Transfer to a bowl and cover with plastic wrap, pressing plastic directly onto surface of pudding. Refrigerate until cold, 1½ hours; pudding will thicken as it cools.

3 Divide half of pudding among 4 parfait glasses. Sprinkle with half of cookies. Repeat with remaining pudding and cookies.

PER SERVING: 401 Cal., 18g Fat (10g Sat.), 75mg Chol., 1g Fiber, 1g Pro., 54g Carb., 200mg Sod.

Kitchen tip

※ **Change the flavor.** Chocolate-sandwich cookies are classic, but other cookies work just as well in this dessert. Try gingersnaps or crisp oatmeal cookies.

Raspberry–White Chocolate Cheesecake Bars

Prep: 35 min.
Bake: 1 hr. 15 min.
Chill: 2 hr.
Yield: 9 bars
Cost per serving:

$1.73

- 1 9-oz. box chocolate wafer cookies
- 5 Tbsp. unsalted butter, melted
- 1 cup frozen raspberries, thawed
- ¼ cup plus 2 Tbsp. sugar
- 16 oz. cream cheese, at room temperature
- 2 large eggs plus 2 large yolks

- 1 Tbsp. flour
- 1 tsp. vanilla extract
- 4 oz. white chocolate, melted and cooled

1 Preheat oven to 350°F. Crush cookies in food processor. Blend in butter. Pour crumbs into a 9-inch pan and press onto bottom and ½ inch up sides. Bake for 8 minutes. Let cool completely. Reduce oven temperature to 250°F.

2 In processor, blend berries and 1 Tbsp. sugar until smooth. Strain; discard solids. Beat cream cheese and remaining sugar until smooth. Beat in eggs and yolks one at a time. Mix in flour and vanilla. Fold in chocolate.

3 Pour cheesecake mixture over crust. Drop spoonfuls of berry puree on top; using a toothpick, drag puree through batter. Bake until cheesecake is just set in center, about 1 hour and 15 minutes. Let cool on a rack, cover and chill for at least 2 hours. Cut and serve.

PER SERVING (1 BAR): 497 Cal., 34g Fat (20g Sat.), 172mg Chol., 2g Fiber, 9g Pro., 41g Carb., 374mg Sod.

*Cookies-and-Cream
Pudding Parfaits*

Index

all*you

Editor **Clare McHugh**
Creative Director **Brenda E. Angelilli**
Deputy Editor **George Kimmerling**
Food Director **Beth Lipton**
Style Director **Carole Nicksin**
Photo Editor **Mercedes Vizcaino**
Senior Editor (Style) **Dwyer Paulsen**
Associate Editor (Food) **Cecily McAndrews**
Associate Art Director **Danielle Avraham**
Associate Photo Editor **Linh Luu-Chan**
Assistant Managing Editor **Jamie Roth Major**
Copy Chief **Mark Yawdoszyn**
Copy Editor **Elizabeth Rhodes**
Production Coordinator **Meaghan Conklin**

Group Publisher **Diane Oshin**
Publisher **Suzanne Quint**
Integrated Marketing Director **Melanie Oliva Shambaugh**
Integrated Marketing Manager **Marianne Bakija**
Publishing Coordinator **Mary Therese Bock**
PR Director **Jennifer Zawadzinski**
Production Manager **George Woods Jr.**
Production Coordinator **Matthew Salvador**
VP Finance **Jennifer Walsh**

Oxmoor House®

VP, Publishing Director **Jim Childs**
Editorial Director **Leah McLaughlin**
Creative Director **Felicity Keane**
Brand Manager **Nina Fleishman**
Senior Editors **Rebecca Brennan, Heather Averett, Andrea C. Kirkland, MS, RD**
Managing Editor **Rebecca Benton**

Time HOME ENTERTAINMENT

Publisher **Richard Fraiman**
VP, Strategy and Business Development **Steven Sandonato**
Executive Director, Marketing Services **Carol Pittard**
Executive Director, Retail and Special Sales **Tom Mifsud**
Executive Publishing Director **Joy Butts**
Editorial Director **Stephen Koepp**
Editorial Operations Director **Michael Q. Bullerdick**
Director, Bookazine Development and Marketing **Laura Adam**
Finance Director **Glenn Buonocore**
Associate Publishing Director **Megan Pearlman**
General Counsel **Helen Wan**

ISBN 10: 0-8487-3816-0
ISBN 13: 978-0-8487-3816-7

First printing 2012

Printed in the United States of America

To order additional publications, call 800-765-6400 or 800-491-0551.

For more books to enrich your life, visit oxmoorhouse.com.

To search, savor and share thousands of recipes, visit myrecipes.com.